Civil Rights
The Struggle for Black Equality

Titles in the
Words That Changed History series include:

The Declaration of Independence
The Emancipation Proclamation
The King James Bible
The Liberator
The Nuremberg Laws
The Origin of Species
Uncle Tom's Cabin
The U.S. Constitution

Words THAT CHANGED HISTORY

Civil Rights
The Struggle for Black Equality

by Charles George

Lucent Books
P.O. Box 289011, San Diego, CA 92198-9011

Library of Congress Cataloging-in-Publication Data

George, Charles, 1949–
   Civil rights : the struggle for black equality / by Charles George
      p. cm. — (Words that changed history)
Includes bibliographical references and index.
   ISBN 1-56006-799-3 (alk. paper)
   1. Afro-Americans—Civil rights—History—Juvenile literature.
   2. Afro-Americans—Civil rights—History—Sources—Juvenile literature.
   3. Afro-American civil rights workers—Biography—Juvenile literature.
   4. Afro-American political activists—Biography—Juvenile literature.
   5. Civil rights movements—United States—History—Juvenile literature.
   6. United States—Race relations—Juvenile literature. [1. Civil rights
movements. 2. Race relations. 3. Civil rights workers. 4. Afro-Americans—
Biography.] I. Title. II. Series.
   E185.61 .G286 2001

                                                                  00–009901

Copyright 2001 by Lucent Books, Inc.
P.O. Box 289011, San Diego, California 92198-9011

No part of this book may be reproduced or used in any other form or by any
other means, electrical, mechanical, or otherwise, including, but not limited to,
photocopy, recording, or any information storage and retrieval system, without
prior written permission from the publisher.

Printed in the U.S.A.

Contents

FOREWORD	6
INTRODUCTION Free in Name Only	8
CHAPTER 1 Compromise and Economic Well-Being	12
CHAPTER 2 The Legal Battle for Civil Rights	26
CHAPTER 3 Nonviolence as a Weapon for Civil Rights	42
CHAPTER 4 The Fight for a Political Voice	57
CHAPTER 5 Rejection of Integration	72
Appendix	86
Source Notes	106
For Further Reading	111
Works Consulted	114
Index	123
Picture Credits	128
About the Author	128

Foreword

"We hold these truths to be self-evident, that all men are created equal, that they are endowed by their Creator with certain unalienable Rights, that among these are Life, Liberty and the pursuit of Happiness." So states one of America's most cherished documents, the Declaration of Independence. These words ripple through time. They represent the thoughts of the Declaration's author, Thomas Jefferson, but at the same time they reflect the attitudes of a nation in which individual rights were trampled by a foreign government. To many of Jefferson's contemporaries, these words characterized a revolutionary philosophy of liberty. Many Americans today still believe the ideas expressed in the Declaration were uniquely American. And while it is true that this document was a product of American ideals and values, its ideas did not spring from an intellectual vacuum. The Enlightenment which had pervaded France and England for years had proffered ideas of individual rights, and Enlightenment scholars drew their notions from historical antecedents tracing back to ancient Greece.

In essence, the Declaration was part of an ongoing historical dialogue concerning the conflict between individual rights and government powers. There is no doubt, however, that it made a palpable impact on its times. For colonists, the Declaration listed their grievances and set out the ideas for which they would stand and fight. These words changed history for Americans. But the Declaration also changed history for other nations; in France, revolutionaries would emulate concepts of self-rule to bring down their own monarchy and draft their own philosophies in a document known as the Declaration of the Rights of Man and of the Citizen. And the historical dialogue continues today in many third world nations.

Lucent's Words That Changed History series looks at oral and written documents in light of their historical context and their lasting impact. Some documents, such as the Declaration, spurred people to immediately change society; other documents fostered lasting intellectual debate. For example, Charles Darwin's treatise *On the Origin of Species* did not simply extend the discussion of human origins; it offered a theory of evolution, which eventually would cause a schism between some religious and scientific thinkers. The debate still rages as people on both sides reaffirm their intellectual positions, even as new scientific evidence continues to impact the issue.

Students researching famous documents, the time periods in which they were prominent, or the issues they raise will find the books in this series both compelling and useful. Readers will see the chain of events that give rise to historical events. They will understand through the examination of specific documents that ideas or philosophies always have their antecedents, and they will learn how these documents carried on the legacy of influence by affecting people in other places or other times. The format for the series emphasizes these points by devoting chapters to the political or intellectual climate of the times, the values and prejudices of the drafters or speakers, the contents of the document and its impact on its contemporaries, and the manner in which perceptions of the document have changed through time.

In addition to their format, the books in Lucent's Words That Changed History series contain features that enhance understanding. Many primary and secondary source quotes give readers insight into the thoughts of the document's contemporaries as well as those who interpret the document's significance in hindsight. Sidebars interspersed throughout the text offer greater examination of relevant personages or significant events to provide readers with a broader historical context. Footnotes allow readers to verify the credibility of source material. Two bibliographies give students the opportunity to expand their research. And an appendix that includes excerpts as well as full text of original documents gives students access to the larger historical picture into which these documents fit.

History is often shaped by words. Oral and written documents concretize the thoughts of a select few, but they often transform the beliefs of an entire era or nation. As Confucius asserted, "Without knowing the force of words, it is impossible to know men." And understanding the power of words reveals a new way of understanding history.

Introduction

Free in Name Only

Equality, freedom, and human dignity are all ideals that Americans hold dear. For African Americans, though, these ideals were for many years unfulfilled. In fact, for much of this nation's history, blacks were relegated to the lowest rungs of the social, economic, and political ladder. First under slavery and then under the system of segregation and discrimination that existed from the end of Reconstruction until the 1960s, African Americans were deprived of the civil rights that white Americans took for granted.

How to gain the rights enshrined in the Declaration of Independence and the Constitution has long been a subject of debate. Accepting the system as it was and fighting it through various means—legal action in the courts, peaceful protest, political activism, and armed rebellion—have all been proposed as the best pathway to achieve equality, but the road has been long—and difficult.

Freedom, but Not Equality

President Abraham Lincoln's Emancipation Proclamation, made effective January 1, 1863, was meant to address—in part, at least—the question of how blacks fit into American society by officially declaring the slaves in the Confederacy free. Not until 1865, though, with the end of the Civil War and the passage of the Thirteenth Amendment to the U.S. Constitution, did African Americans throughout the nation actually gain their freedom. But freedom was not the same as equality, and the question of the status of blacks remained unresolved.

Two further amendments to the Constitution were supposed to guarantee equality for blacks. The Fourteenth, ratified in 1868, provided for "equal protection" of the law for all citizens, and the Fifteenth, ratified in 1870, was intended to ensure that African Americans had voting rights. But the amendments did not have the desired effects.

Eventually, Northerners lost interest in the social reforms that the Reconstruction period was meant to bring about in the South after the Civil War. Settlement of the American West became the nation's focus, rather than rehabilitation of the former Confederacy. In 1877, Reconstruction officially came to an end, ending federal supervision of the South and completely returning local control to the former Confederate states.

The Arrival of Jim Crow

Before long, however, blacks saw much of what they had gained erode. From 1877 until the turn of the twentieth century, white Southern politicians methodically revoked blacks' newly won rights through state laws, local ordinances, economic pressure, and outright intimidation. Ignoring constitutional guarantees, the South initiated laws to separate blacks from whites. These were called Jim Crow laws, after a stereotypical black character in a derogatory song in a nineteenth-century Southern minstrel show. This system of laws and social customs continued well past the midpoint of the twentieth century.

Well into the 1960s, blacks were systematically excluded from mainstream American life. Most black children were relegated to poorly built, improperly maintained and equipped schools instead of being allowed to attend white schools. Access to public facilities, which were paid for by tax revenue collected from all citizens, including African Americans, was severely limited or forbidden to blacks.

Blacks in the South, and in many parts of the North as well, could not attend state universities or sit in certain sections of buses and trains. Dining rooms, public swimming pools, parks, and theaters were all strictly segregated. White hospitals refused to admit black patients, and many white doctors would not treat black patients. Conversely, black doctors were not allowed to treat whites. Churches, department stores, and even

President Abraham Lincoln signed the Emancipation Proclamation on January 1, 1863, officially freeing slaves in the Confederacy.

Under Jim Crow laws, black children had to attend segregated schools like this one in White Plains, Georgia.

cemeteries were segregated. Strictly enforced Jim Crow laws and long-standing social customs ensured that African Americans would remain second-class citizens.

Barriers to Voting

Other measures were designed to ensure that the second-class status of blacks would endure. Knowing that blacks were in the majority in many areas of the South, whites felt it crucial just after Reconstruction to limit access to the polls only to themselves, thereby keeping blacks powerless to change the system. Finding loopholes in the Fourteenth and Fifteenth Amendments, Southern politicians instituted various barriers to stop African Americans from voting.

First, they levied a poll tax, to be paid by prospective voters when they registered—usually around five dollars, which was prohibitively expensive for blacks, who often earned from forty cents to two dollars a day.

Other restrictions passed into law by Southern states included the "understanding clause" and the "good character clause." Potential voters had to demonstrate to county officials that they could read and understand some written document—usually a portion of the state constitution. The former slaves had generally received little education, so few could pass this test. Even if an African American could read and interpret the assigned passage, it was up to the registrar of voters to judge whether someone had passed the test. That same official also had the authority to deny registration to any applicant on the basis of his judgment of the applicant's moral character.

To make certain that such rules would affect only African Americans, most states included another provision, the "grandfather clause." Persons who had been able to vote on January 1, 1867, along with their direct descendants, were exempted from the various tests and allowed to vote. Since only a tiny percentage of African Americans had been able to vote at that time, almost all of them were subject to the rigorous tests.

During this period, African Americans were not equal in school, at work, or anywhere else in society. As a result, black leaders continued the struggle to gain equal rights. Opinions varied, however, on how these rights were to be won.

Different Pathways to the Same Goal

No matter which pathway was taken, the goal remained the same. The United States of America, from its inception, has claimed to stand for certain noble principles, including equal rights for all people. Whether through compromise, legal strategy, peaceful protest, the vote, or a more militant approach, African Americans have struggled for what should have been theirs from the outset—an equal share in the nation's promise.

CHAPTER 1
Compromise and Economic Well-Being

On September 18, 1895, Booker T. Washington, principal of the Tuskegee Institute in Alabama, delivered a speech at the opening of the Cotton States and International Exposition in Atlanta, Georgia. His address, calling for cooperation between the races in exchange for an increase in vocational training for African Americans, set the tone for race relations in the United States for decades to come. Washington, like other black leaders, wanted better conditions for black Americans and believed that his strategy would accomplish that goal.

According to historian Henry Steele Commager, most white Southerners at the time thought that blacks were making great progress, especially when their post-Reconstruction situation was compared to slavery. In their opinion, blacks should be satisfied with that progress, no matter how slowly it came, and should not agitate for anything more. It was the white Southerners' position that

Booker T. Washington believed vocational training was the best way for African Americans to improve their economic and political condition.

evolution was better than revolution, and . . . that evolution was a slow process, and they did not understand why Negroes should not take the same satisfaction in gradual evolution as they did. Basic to their attitude was one explicit and one implicit assumption. The explicit assumption was that Southerners knew best—the Southern white, that is—and that race relations would take care of themselves if only outsiders, e.g., Northerners, would leave the South alone. The implicit assumption—which was explicit enough under pressure—was that the Negro was after all inferior to the white, and that he should not therefore expect genuine equality, political, economic, or social.[1]

In a time when lynchings and other forms of intimidation were commonplace, public demonstrations, boycotts, and other forms of direct protest were simply too dangerous and became almost unheard of in the South. Instead, a philosophy of accommodation came to the forefront. This strategy favored giving in to white society's restrictions in an effort to create goodwill between the races. It was believed that, over time, whites would gradually come to respect African Americans as a result of their hard work and cooperation with "the system."

A Practical Approach

The most prominent spokesman for this philosophy was Booker T. Washington, but the basis for his thinking goes back much further than his own time.

As early as the 1840s, Frederick Douglass, one of the most brilliant and influential African Americans of the day, argued for the establishment of trade schools. Douglass, a former slave, was editor of his own abolitionist newspaper, *The North Star*, a gifted lecturer, and a tireless worker for the abolition of slavery. Looking ahead to a time when slavery would end, Douglass and other black leaders believed that a policy of self-help and trade schools would increase the value of blacks to Southern society, and thus, at some time in the distant future, blacks would win the respect of white Southerners.

With the establishment of the Freedmen's Bureau in 1865, just before the end of the Civil War, schools for Southern blacks became a reality. Most freedmen's schools focused their efforts on industrial or vocational education and, according to historian Milton Meltzer, urged black students:

> [H]elp yourself—with white guidance—and you will acquire property and high moral standards. Along the road, somewhere in the dim future, the blessings of full citizenship will be bestowed upon you.[2]

The Freedmen's Bureau

Toward the end of the Civil War, former slaves and free blacks appealed for aid to Northerners and abolitionists, who pressured Congress to provide help. In March 1865, the Bureau of Refugees, Freedmen, and Abandoned Lands, more popularly known as the Freedmen's Bureau, was established. In the five years of its existence, the Freedmen's Bureau provided food, clothing, supplies, job placement, education, and land to freed slaves and white refugees of the war.

One of its main goals, to set up schools in the South, was quite successful. Aided by religious and philanthropic groups, it founded 4,300 schools, from elementary level through college. Over 250,000 blacks started their education in Freedmen's Bureau schools, taught by volunteer teachers from the North.

The Influence of Hampton

It was to one of these freedmen's schools, Hampton Normal and Industrial Institute, that young Booker T. Washington came. His years at Hampton, first as student and later as teacher, would have a profound effect on his philosophy.

At the age of fourteen, Washington heard about Hampton Institute from coworkers in a salt mine near his home in Malden, West Virginia. Determined to get an education, he set out in 1872 for Hampton, Virginia, to attend school.

Hampton, established in 1868, had been the idea of Samuel Chapman Armstrong, a son of missionaries and a former general in the Union Army. After the war, Armstrong became an agent of the Freedmen's Bureau. In 1866, he took charge of a huge camp of former slaves in Hampton, Virginia. The following year, seeing the need for former slaves to receive an education, he convinced the American Missionary Association and a private benefactor to purchase land and establish a vocational institution there.

Armstrong thought that vocational training rather than traditional education would be more acceptable to Southern whites who had feared the education of blacks since the days of slavery. He taught his students that economic advancement should be the goal of blacks instead of political or social equality. He urged students and faculty to accept the loss of such civil rights as voting and serving on juries in return for the opportunity to learn a trade.

Booker T. Washington considered Armstrong "the noblest, rarest human being that it has ever been my privilege to meet."[3] In addition to Armstrong, other teachers at Hampton also influenced Washington. One, Miss Nathalie Lord, helped him develop his speaking abilities through the Hampton debating societies. She also instilled in him an understanding of the use and value of the Bible. The Christian ideas of "turn the other cheek" and "love your neighbor" helped form Washington's conciliatory attitude toward Southern whites.

Another faculty member, Principal Mary F. Mackie, repeatedly demonstrated to Washington the importance and dignity of labor. Despite her education and social standing, she insisted upon working alongside students when they prepared the school each year for the new term—washing windows, dusting rooms, making beds, doing whatever was required.

Washington later wrote of his experience at Hampton:

> At Hampton, I not only learned that it was not a disgrace to labour, but learned to love labour, not alone for its financial value, but for labour's own sake and for the independence and self-reliance which the ability to do something which the world wants done brings. At that institution I got my first taste of what it meant to live a life of unselfishness, my first knowledge of the fact that the happiest individuals are those who do the most to make others useful and happy.[4]

Samuel Chapman Armstrong was founder of the Hampton Normal and Industrial Institute, where Booker T. Washington attended school.

The Beginnings of Tuskegee

Working his way through Hampton Institute as a janitor and waiter, Washington completed his studies in 1875. A few years later, he returned to Hampton as an instructor. In the interim, he had studied at Wayland Seminary, in Washington, D.C., an institution with no vocational training program. Washington considered students there to be less self-reliant than those at Hampton:

They [students at Wayland] seemed to give more attention to mere outward appearances. In a word, they did not appear to me to be beginning at the bottom, on a real, solid foundation, to the extent that they were at Hampton. They knew more about Latin and Greek when they left school, but they seemed to know less about life and its conditions as they would meet it at their homes.[5]

In 1881, General Armstrong, in response to a letter from businessmen in Alabama, suggested Washington as the head of another voca-

The Tuskegee Institute

In Tuskegee, Alabama, Booker T. Washington and his associates turned a run-down shanty and an old church building into a world famous school for African Americans. When it opened on July 4, 1881, its first thirty students sat in a classroom where the roof leaked so badly that they had to hold umbrellas over their heads when it rained.

Tuskegee's male students learned trades such as farming, carpentry, and blacksmithing. Female students were taught cooking, sewing, and housekeeping. In addition to vocational subjects, students were also taught etiquette and respect for the rights of others, in keeping with Washington's belief in strict discipline and the role of education in developing character.

By 1915, the year of Washington's death, the Institute had more than one hundred buildings on 2,000 acres of land. It boasted an endowment of $2,000,000, an annual budget of over $250,000, a faculty of 197, and a student body of 1,537. In 1985 the Institute became Tuskegee University. It now has 3,200 students, pursuing degrees in business, agriculture, engineering, and numerous other fields, but has retained its mission of preparing its students to earn the respect of others by excelling in their chosen careers.

Students attend a history class at the Tuskegee Institute in 1902.

The organizers of the Atlanta Exposition decided to devote an entire building to showcasing contributions African Americans had made to Southern agriculture and industry.

tional school for blacks in Tuskegee. Starting with little more than an old shack and an abandoned church, Washington used what he had learned from General Armstrong to create a major educational institution. In the process, because of the success of the "Tuskegee Movement," he made a name for himself.

The Road to Atlanta and National Acclaim

Washington became a much sought-after speaker on the subject of race and the importance of education for blacks. In 1894, prominent citizens in Atlanta invited him to join a mostly white delegation to testify before a congressional committee about the need for an agricultural exposition in the South to showcase its progress since the Civil War. Washington's testimony, along with that of others in the delegation, convinced Congress to approve a federal grant-in-aid to fund the event.

Directors of the exposition, aware of the role that African Americans had played in the success of the South, decided to recognize the agricultural and industrial contributions of blacks. They voted to include a building devoted entirely to blacks, designed and built by African Americans.

In addition, because of the prominent role to be played by blacks in the exposition, the board of directors also decided to invite a representative of the black people to speak at the opening ceremonies. After days of discussion, they voted unanimously to ask Booker T. Washington to speak.

An Important Choice of Words

His invitation did not limit what he could include in his speech, and that fact made his sense of responsibility weigh even more heavily upon him. Newspapers in the North and the South reported the board's decision to allow him to speak, and a good many white Southerners were opposed to the prospect. Because of this opposition, Washington decided that his speech should give encouragement to blacks, and, at the same time, soothe the apprehensions, fears, and suspicions of whites.

Everyone seemed to have a suggestion as to what he ought to say. In the end, though, Washington had to be true to his personal philosophy. He believed that blacks needed to have patience in the slow, gradual improvement of their status in American society. He also wanted them to see the importance of vocational education and the dignity of hard work.

Washington's Assessment of the Situation

His 1895 speech in Atlanta, one of the first major addresses by an African American to a predominantly white Southern audience, spelled out his strategy. Gradual economic progress, rather than drastic political activism, was the best course to follow. By establishing themselves as productive citizens of the South, with property and the respect of white Southerners, blacks would eventually "earn" those political rights.

One of the main points made by Washington seemed to reinforce the belief of Southern whites in their racial superiority. He stated that white Southerners should be commended, not criticized, for their paternalistic view of African Americans. In the original draft of the speech he wrote:

> We must admit the stern fact that at present the Negro, through no choice of his own, is living among another race which is far ahead of him in education, property, experience, and favourable condition; further, that the Negro's present condition makes him dependent upon the white people for most of the things necessary to sustain life, as well as for his common school education.[6]

In his view, blacks were not able to compete equally with whites in the workplace, because of their inexperience and lack of education, and therefore were doomed to fail unless aided by white society.

He also noted that vocational education was the key to the success of blacks:

> The Negro in the South has it within his power, if he properly utilises the forces at hand, to make of himself such a valuable factor in the life of the South that he will not have to seek privileges, they will be freely conferred upon him. To bring this

Students participate in a weaving class. Weaving was just one of the many trades taught at the Tuskegee Institute.

about, the Negro must begin at the bottom and lay a sure foundation.[7]

Concerning the political rights promised in the Constitution, Washington was optimistic, at least over the long term, about the prospects for blacks:

> I believe that, speaking of his future in general terms, he [a black person] will be treated with justice, will be given the protection of the law, and will be given the recognition in a large measure which his usefulness and ability warrant.[8]

He made few changes of any importance from the first draft to the final version of the speech that he delivered on that hot September day. Intense heat and tremendous crowds in Atlanta added to his nervousness. The city was packed with people from around the country and representatives from foreign governments, military, and civic organizations. Thousands awaited the opening ceremonies.

Shortly after the program began, Washington addressed the packed auditorium. He later wrote:

When I arose to speak, there was considerable cheering, especially from the coloured people. As I remember it now, the thing that was uppermost in my mind was the desire to say something that would cement the friendship of the races and bring about hearty cooperation between them.[9]

"Cast Down Your Bucket"

In his fifteen-minute address, Washington spoke at times to white Southerners in the audience and at other times to those African Americans present. To whites, he conceded his love for the South and his understanding of Southern ways. To blacks, he urged patience, hard work, cooperation, and goodwill toward white Southerners.

His speech has been called the "Cast Down Your Bucket" speech because of his use of an often-told story of a ship lost at sea off the coast of South America. The crew members of the unfortunate vessel, having run out of drinking water, were dying of thirst. Not realizing that they were sailing in the current of fresh water pouring from the mouth of the Amazon River, they would have died if the captain of a passing vessel had not called to them to cast down their bucket where they were.

Washington used this story to illustrate several points in his speech. Convinced that blacks could succeed better in the rural South, he urged African Americans in the audience to remain there rather than migrate to the urban North. Washington believed that they would encounter a culture in the North unfamiliar to them, making it harder for them to fit in:

In his speech to the Atlanta Exposition, Washington invited both blacks and whites to "Cast Down Your Bucket" in order to make use of resources they already possessed.

To those of my race who depend upon bettering their condition in a foreign land [the North], or who underestimate the importance of cultivating friendly relations with the Southern white man, who is his next door neighbor, I would say: "Cast down your bucket where you are"—cast it down in making friends in every manly way of the people of all races by whom we are surrounded.

He also urged blacks to concentrate their economic efforts in familiar fields of labor. Sharing his respect for manual labor and his feelings about the dignity of common laborers, he said:

> Cast it down in agriculture, mechanics, in commerce, in domestic service, and in the professions. . . . Our greatest danger is that in the great leap from slavery to freedom we may overlook the fact that the masses of us are to live by the productions of our hands, and fail to keep in mind that we shall prosper in proportion as we learn to dignify and glorify common labor. . . . No race can prosper till it learns that there is as much dignity in tilling a field as in writing a poem.[10]

Using the same analogy, he also addressed whites in the audience, suggesting that they should consider the black population of the South, rather than immigrants who had recently arrived from Europe, as partners for a brighter future.

Reminding his white listeners of the importance of slave labor before the Civil War, Washington urged them to look to the eight million African Americans who were their neighbors as a source of skilled labor:

> Cast down your bucket among these people who have, without strikes and labor wars, tilled your fields, cleared your forests, builded your railroads and cities, and brought forth treasures from the bowels of the earth, and helped make possible this magnificent representation of the progress of the South. Casting down your bucket among my people, helping and encouraging them as you are doing on these grounds, and, with education of head, hand, and heart, you will find that they will buy your surplus land, make blossom the waste places in your fields, and run your factories.[11]

In his conclusion, he assured Southern whites that, in exchange for their support in providing vocational education for blacks in the South, blacks would abandon, or at least postpone, demands for equality in civil rights. Amid rousing cheers from the predominantly white audience, he declared:

> The wisest among my race understand that the agitation of questions of social equality is the extremest of folly, and that progress in the enjoyment of all the privileges that will come to us must be the result of severe and constant struggle rather than of artificial forcing. . . . It is important and right that all

privileges of the law be ours, but it is vastly more important that we be prepared for the exercise of these privileges.[12]

Because of its conciliatory nature, Booker T. Washington's speech has also been referred to as the "Atlanta Compromise" speech.

The Voice of Compromise Draws Immediate Praise

Response to the speech was immediate. James Creelman, newspaperman and author, reported in the New York *World* the next day:

> Within ten minutes the multitude was in an uproar of enthusiasm, handkerchiefs were waved, canes were flourished, hats were tossed in the air. The fairest women of Georgia stood up and cheered. It was as if the orator had bewitched them. . . . And when he held his dusky hand high above his head, with the fingers stretched wide apart, and said to the white people of the South on behalf of his race: "In all things that are purely social we can be as separate as the fingers, yet one as the hand in all things essential to social progress" the great wave of sound bashed itself against the walls and the whole audience was on its feet in a delirium of applause. . . .[13]

Relieved by the message of accommodation, ex-Governor of Georgia Rufus B. Bullock, a former slaveholder and Confederate officer, rushed across the stage to shake Washington's hand. The American president, Grover Cleveland, joined hundreds of others in praising Washington, first sending a congratulatory telegram and then personally visiting the Atlanta Exposition.

Newspapers across the country hailed the speech, calling Booker T. Washington "one of the great men of the South," "a prominent and sensible man," and "a progressive negro educator."[14] Response to his speech by a white America pleased with the idea of a compliant, cooperative, yet well-trained domestic work force thrust Washington into the position of spokesman for black Americans.

From the moment he finished his address in Atlanta until his death in 1915, he remained one of the most powerful men in America, black or white. Presidents Cleveland and Theodore Roosevelt looked to him for advice. Philanthropists and industrial giants, such as Andrew Carnegie and John D. Rockefeller, also sought his counsel.

Voices of Discontent

Despite honors, praise, and recognition heaped on Washington, not everyone agreed with his philosophy. In 1902, one black editorialist, William Monroe Trotter, noted in the Boston *Guardian* the lack of progress in the status of African Americans in the South since Washington's speech. He criticized Washington's apparent lack of concern for the loss of black voting rights and for the lack of black representation at state constitutional conventions:

> No thinking Negro can fail to see that, with the influence Mr. Washington yields [wields] in the North and the confidence reposed in him by the white people on account of his school, a fatal blow has been given to the Negro's political rights and liberty by his statement.

President Grover Cleveland was one of many who praised Washington's speech.

O, for a black Patrick Henry to save his people from this stigma of cowardice; . . . to inspire his people with the spirit of those immortal words: "Give Me Liberty or Give Me Death."[15]

Washington's most prominent critic, W. E. B. Du Bois, initially praised the Atlanta speech. In his 1903 book *The Souls of Black Folk*, however, he soundly criticized Washington's approach. More than five years after the delivery of the speech, Du Bois observed that the status of blacks in the South had, in fact, deteriorated. He cited an increase in the number of African Americans being lynched, the virtual peonage (being forced to serve a master to pay off a debt) of rural Southern blacks, and the almost regionwide disfranchisement (deprivation of rights) of the race.

Du Bois, a Harvard-educated scholar, was also disheartened by the nation's educational policy toward African Americans. He had always seen higher education as the best solution for bringing blacks to an equal level with whites. Washington's national prominence, however, brought financial backing for vocational schools while completely overshadowing the need for black colleges and universities.

Du Bois continued to oppose Washington, blaming him for antiblack attitudes held by many whites during the Jim Crow era. He also thought that, instead of freeing African Americans from oppression, Washington's gradualism served only to perpetuate it—this was too high a price to pay for vocational training.

According to Thomas E. Harris, author of a scholarly analysis of the debate between these two black leaders:

> Washington sought accommodation for a price. Du Bois and his followers, both at the time and since, labeled the price too high and have labeled the Alabama educator a collaborator who sold his race down the river.[16]

Another critic, black minister Charles Satchel Morris, while not questioning Washington's motives, said in 1906:

> I believe Booker T. Washington's heart is right, but that in fawning, cringing, and groveling before the white man he has cost his race their rights and that twenty years hence, as he looks back and sees the harm his course has done his race, he will be brokenhearted over it.[17]

The Legacy of Compromise

Washington never adopted Morris's view, but in later years he modified his views somewhat. He spoke out for political rights, criticizing a sys-

W. E. B. Du Bois (1868–1963)

William Edward Burghardt Du Bois was a historian, sociologist, writer, and civil rights activist. Some have called him the foremost African American intellectual of the twentieth century.

Born in Great Barrington, Massachusetts, he was educated at Fisk University, Harvard (where he was the first African American to earn a doctorate from the university), and the University of Berlin. Over his long and illustrious career, Du Bois published nineteen books, including his most outstanding, *The Souls of Black Folk (1903)*, in which he criticized what he saw as the accomodationist policies of Booker T. Washington.

In 1905 he cofounded the Niagara Movement, an organization of black intellectuals who wanted to fight for black civil rights and to oppose Washington's approach. Du Bois was also one of the founding officers of the National Association for the Advancement of Colored People (NAACP), serving as editor of its monthly magazine *The Crisis*. Disillusioned with American racism, he settled in the African nation of Ghana in 1961, where he died in 1963.

Pictured with industrialist Andrew Carnegie (seated, front row, second from right), is the 1902 faculty of the Tuskegee Institute. Washington is seated to Carnegie's right.

tem under which blacks paid taxes but were not allowed to vote. Despite this change in his views, Washington never abandoned his devotion to vocational education as the best method for achieving economic advancement for blacks.

Today, most African Americans believe that Washington's "Atlanta Compromise" speech contributed to the continuation of a social order in the South that virtually reenslaved African Americans and required more than a half-century to overcome. Not until the "Second Reconstruction," when black soldiers returned from serving in World War II, did demands for progress toward racial equality begin to make an impact.

CHAPTER 2
The Legal Battle for Civil Rights

On Monday, May 17, 1954, Chief Justice Earl Warren read the decision of the Supreme Court in the matter of *Brown v. the Board of Education of Topeka, Kansas*. The Court's opinion included the words ". . . in the field of public education the doctrine of 'separate but equal' has no place."[18] These fifteen words sparked a national furor. They overturned *Plessy v. Ferguson*, the 1896 Court ruling that had established the legality of racial segregation, and capped a twenty-three-year concentrated effort by lawyers of the National Association for the Advancement of Colored People (NAACP) to end segregation in American education.

Faith in the Law

Whereas Booker T. Washington, in his "Atlanta Compromise" speech, advocated a policy of cooperation and concentration on economic advancement in order to achieve equality for African Americans, other blacks believed that whites would treat blacks as equals only if blacks were first legally recognized as equals. Among those most insistent on this strategy were two attorneys, Charles Hamilton Houston and his protégé, Thurgood Marshall.

Marshall was chief counsel in the *Brown* case and served as director of the Legal Defense Fund (LDF), the legal arm of the NAACP. Houston had been dean of the Howard University Law School and, in 1935, became the NAACP's first full-time legal staff member. At Howard, he taught his students that, regardless of the many state and local segregation laws, and the previous Supreme Court decisions to the contrary, the Constitution—particularly the Fourteenth and Fifteenth Amendments—guaranteed equal rights to *all* Americans and could be made to work for African Americans.

The strategy of using America's own legal system to gain civil rights for African Americans was based on a firm belief that the U.S. Congress and state legislatures would not take the action needed to guarantee equality for blacks. For most of the early decades of the twentieth century, Southern Democrats stymied the passage of any meaningful civil rights legislation. Despite the 1896 Supreme Court ruling in *Plessy v. Ferguson*, some blacks hoped justice could be found in the court system. One observer wrote in 1935 that blacks "*can* resort to the courts with a reasonable certainty of favorable decisions. . . . [Blacks] *must* resort to the courts. They have no other reasonable, legitimate alternative."[19] The Supreme Court, then, became the only avenue for relief from racial discrimination. In the Court, political considerations were supposed to be secondary to the law of the land, and regional prejudice was supposed to be absent.

The Garland Fund

From its founding in 1909, the NAACP had supported lawsuits to combat segregation, but lack of sufficient funds made that pursuit difficult and rather sporadic. In the late 1920s, a left-wing organization—the American Fund for Public Service—proposed giving the NAACP a grant of several hundred thousand dollars to pursue such legal cases.

Also called the Garland Fund, after its chief benefactor, Charles Garland, its main goal was the education and organization into labor unions of America's workers. Because the nation's twelve million blacks constituted the largest group of unorganized workers in the United States, the Fund's Committee on Negro Work voted to initiate

> a large-scale, widespread, dramatic campaign to give the Southern Negro his constitutional rights, his political and civil equality,

Thurgood Marshall (pictured, fourth from left, with the NAACP's legal team), believed that blacks could gain equality by working through the courts.

and therewith a self-consciousness and self-respect which would inevitably tend to effect a revolution in the economic life of the country.[20]

Along with the grant came a memorandum proposing an overall legal strategy to accomplish this goal, especially in the field of education. The committee suggested funding lawsuits by local taxpayers to challenge the equality of segregated schools in seven Southern states where discrimination was most blatant: Alabama, Arkansas, Florida, Georgia, Louisiana, Mississippi, and South Carolina.

The suits would demand that facilities for blacks be brought up to the standard of those for whites. Since this was the core of the "separate but equal" philosophy in the law, the committee members believed the financial burden of creating truly equal facilities for blacks would force Southern states to abandon the costly dual system and integrate schools. The memorandum also noted that court cases would serve as examples

Under laws passed following the end of Reconstruction, black children were forced to attend schools that were vastly inferior to those attended by white children.

to other African Americans, motivating them to challenge other forms of discrimination.

Nathan Margold and the Margold Report

Finally having the funds needed to battle segregation in the courts, the NAACP, under Executive Secretary Walter White, sought to recruit a lawyer to formulate its battle plan. Needing the best recommendations available for a person to fill such a crucial role, White consulted two of the best legal minds of the day.

First, White consulted Charles Houston. He also talked to Harvard Law School's Felix Frankfurter. Frankfurter, who would later serve on the Supreme Court, had been Houston's mentor. He was also legal counsel to the American Civil Liberties Union (ACLU) and a member of the NAACP legal advisory committee. Both men agreed that Nathan Ross Margold, Houston's classmate and one of Frankfurter's star students at Harvard, would be ideal for the task.

Margold did not fully agree with the Garland Committee's recommendations for legal action. He thought that, since there were thousands of school districts in the South, individual suits challenging the equality of each facility would be inefficient. Proving one district's black schools inferior to its white ones would have no effect on neighboring districts unless state laws that required such segregation were also challenged in state and federal courts. He believed that NAACP lawsuits should focus on state laws requiring separate schools, on unequal expenditures for black and white schools, and on the absence of procedures existing in those state laws to equalize those expenditures.

In view of the Supreme Court's earlier decisions about the rights of African Americans, in *Plessy* and subsequent cases through 1927, it was difficult to see how Margold could think that any relief might be gained from federal courts. In preparing his 218-page document, "The Margold Report," in 1931, however, he discovered that the question of segregated schools had never been confronted directly by the Court. Historian Richard Kluger explains:

> In *Plessy*, Margold contended, the Court had countenanced [approved of] racial segregation only so long as the separate facilities were equal. But what if the facilities were not equal? And what if a state's schools were habitually operated in a way that failed to provide equal educational facilities for Negroes? Neither of these questions challenged the essential legality of segregation itself.[21]

The Margold Report offered two courses of action—lawsuits that would force Southern officials to make black and white schools equal and assertions that inferior schools damaged African American children and made them feel inferior.

As clear as it seemed on paper, the Margold Report's plan was not implemented immediately. The economic realities of the Great Depression, which began in 1929, made financing difficult, especially since the Garland Fund was not able to contribute as much money as it had promised. Not until the mid- to late 1930s was the NAACP able to pursue its goal in the courts.

Charles Hamilton Houston's Strategy

In 1935, Walter White convinced Charles Hamilton Houston to leave Howard University Law School and head the NAACP's legal challenge of segregation. Houston wholeheartedly agreed with Margold's assertion that education was the proper area of focus for the NAACP's campaign. In mid-1935, he outlined the reasons for focusing the majority of the organization's efforts on education:

> Education . . . is preparation for the competition of life. . . . [A] poor education handicaps an individual in the competition. . . . Economically inferior education makes [Negroes] less able to stand competition with whites for jobs. . . . [Inferior education makes it difficult for] young Negro men and women [to be] courageous and aggressive in defense of their rights.[22]

Like his mentor, Felix Frankfurter, Houston believed lawyers had to decide what sort of society they wished to create and then use whatever legal rules were currently in existence as tools to construct that society. As social engineers, Frankfurter said lawyers should use not only existing laws and the courts but also information from sociologists, historians, and other social scientists.

Thurgood Marshall Joins the Fight

Knowing how much work lay ahead, Houston recruited the best, most aggressive legal minds in the country to assist him. First on his list was Thurgood Marshall, who had been one of his top students at Howard University Law School.

Houston, with Marshall and others assisting, decided to focus the NAACP's first cases on segregated graduate schools and law schools. Two facts made higher education cases the logical place to start. Besides Howard University and Meharry Medical College in Nashville, Tennessee, there were no other graduate or professional schools within any black college in the South. In addition, few states provided separate facilities in white universities for blacks at the graduate level. This almost total exclusion of African American students, Houston thought, would make unequal access easy to prove.

Charles Hamilton Houston (1895–1950)

Charles Hamilton Houston was born on September 3, 1895, fifteen days before Booker T. Washington delivered his "Atlanta Compromise" speech and nearly eight months before the Supreme Court ruled, in *Plessy v. Ferguson (1896)*, that separate but equal facilities for blacks were constitutional, thus setting the precedent for segregation. A grandson of a runaway slave, Houston attended segregated schools in Washington, D.C., before being admitted, at age fifteen, to Amherst College in Massachusetts.

Charles Houston's efforts were aimed at ending segregation, particularly in education.

He received his law degree from Harvard Law School in 1923 and joined the faculty of Howard University Law School in the following year. Later, as vice dean at the Howard Law School, Houston created a program in which African American students were taught specific strategies to use in fighting for civil rights in the courts.

In 1934 Houston became director of the NAACP's legal campaign and, through a series of court cases, began chipping away at the legal precedent of "separate but equal" established by the *Plessy* decision. His legal strategy laid the groundwork for future civil rights cases, including *Brown v. Board of Education*. As noted in Columbus Salley's book, *The Black 100: A Ranking of the Most Influential African Americans, Past and Present*, Thurgood Marshall said of his mentor:

> When Brown against the Board of Education was being argued in the Supreme Court . . . [t]here were some dozen lawyers on the side of Negroes fighting for their schools. . . . [O]f those . . . only two hadn't been touched by Charlie Houston. . . . [T]hat man was the engineer of it all. . . . I can tell you this . . . if you do it legally, Charlie Houston made it possible. . . . This is what I think . . . Charlie Houston means to us.

Early Court Cases Set the Tone for Later Victories

The NAACP's first civil rights victory came in 1936. Donald Murray, a young black man, had applied to the law school at the University of Maryland. Denied admittance to the white law school and seeing the university had no separate facility for African Americans, Murray sued. Marshall, who had also been denied entrance to the same law school years earlier because of his race, helped argue the case successfully in the Baltimore city court. The University of Maryland, ordered to admit Murray, complied.

Over the next twelve years, other cases followed. One in particular, *Sipuel v. University of Oklahoma Board of Regents*, brought in 1948, stands out. Ada Sipuel, a graduate of an all-black college, had applied for admission to the University of Oklahoma's law school and had been told instead to attend what on paper was a separate black law school. This "law school," however, had no faculty, no library, and no campus—it was merely a section of the state's capitol building, roped off. Marshall, by now director of the NAACP's Legal Defense Fund (LDF), tried a new approach.

According to Peter Irons, political science professor, civil liberties lawyer, and author:

> Thurgood Marshall . . . argued, for the first time, that segregation was flatly unconstitutional. Even if states provided blacks with better schools than whites, he said, separating them by race imposed a "badge of inferiority" on blacks.[23]

The Court decided that the university had to provide Sipuel with a genuine law school education. By 1949, tiring of court battles, the university admitted her to its law school.

The Background of *Brown*

The "badge of inferiority" referred to in the *Sipuel* case was precisely what Thurgood Marshall and others from the LDF attempted to prove in five separate lawsuits that they eventually brought before the Court, known collectively as *Brown v. Board of Education*. Grouped together because of their similarities, the cases originated in four states and the District of Columbia: *Davis et al. [and others] v. County School Board of Prince Edward County, Virginia*; *Gebhart v. Belton* (Delaware); *Bolling v. Sharpe* (Washington, D.C.); *Brown v. Board of Education of Topeka, Kansas*; and *Briggs v. Elliott* (South Carolina).

In order to demonstrate that segregated schools, whether equal or not, harmed black children, Marshall and the NAACP legal staff had to provide scientific evidence that black children harbored negative self-images resulting from segregation. They invited Dr. Kenneth B. Clark,

Thurgood Marshall (standing, left) looks on as the University of Oklahoma dean of admissions accepts Ada Sipuel's application to the university's law school.

an experimental psychologist from New York, to visit children at the segregated schools. Clark brought with him the tools of his trade—four dolls, two pink and two brown.

Meeting one at a time with black children, he showed them the dolls. When asked to do so, the children easily identified a white or a black doll. But when he asked the children to give him "the nice doll," "the doll you like best," or "the doll you like to play with," most of the children identified the white doll in response to such a request.

His next requests made clear the image that these children had of themselves. When he said, "Give me the doll that looks bad," many children said that the brown doll looked "bad" to them. Having rejected the brown doll, they became upset when he told them, "Give me the doll that looks most like you." Pointing to the same brown doll that he had rejected, one young boy said, "That's the bad one; that's the nigger."[24]

As part of his court strategy, Marshall, according to Peter Irons, wanted to show that

> what made the enforced separation of black children from whites most damaging . . . was not tattered textbooks and untrained

Kenneth B. Clark (1914–)

Psychologist and author Kenneth Bancroft Clark gave expert testimony in the cases known collectively as *Brown v. Board of Education* that helped bring an end to school segregation in America. Born July 24, 1914, in the U.S.-owned Canal Zone in Panama, Clark attended integrated schools in Harlem before receiving bachelor's and master's degrees from Howard University and his doctorate in experimental psychology from Columbia University.

His use of black and white dolls to gauge the effects of discrimination on children's minds arose from personal experience. In the early 1920s, his mother was a follower of Marcus Garvey's teachings which were aimed at fostering black pride. Clark later recounted proudly that his mother went to a great deal of trouble and expense to buy his sister a black doll, rather than a white one, because Garvey stressed the need for black children to have black dolls as an aid to developing positive self-images.

Psychologist Kenneth B. Clark provided crucial support for Marshall's arguments in the Brown v. Board of Education *case.*

teachers, but the stigma of inferiority that segregation inflicted on black children. School officials could buy newer books and hire better teachers for black children, but they could not erase feelings of inferiority from their minds.[25]

Clark's study gave Marshall the ammunition that he needed.

Arguing *Brown* Before the Supreme Court

On December 9, 1953, Marshall, part of a team of LDF lawyers arguing the five individual cases, rose in the Supreme Court to speak on behalf of black children in Clarendon County, South Carolina. According to biographer Juan Williams, he told the justices:

> Inferior schools and resources were not the issue, it was segregation itself. Racial separation hurt the "development of the personalities of [black] children" and "deprived them of equal status in the school community . . . destroying their self-respect." He [Marshall] concluded that the "humiliation" black children went through was "not theoretical injury" but "actual injury."[26]

During the presentation of the NAACP's case, the justices interrupted many times with questions, trying to clarify the issue. At one point, Justice Felix Frankfurter asked Marshall what he meant when he used the word *equal*. He responded with a simple yet profound definition: "Equal means getting the same thing, at the same time and in the same place."[27]

When the opposing lawyer, John W. Davis, argued that states had the right to maintain segregated schools, Marshall responded that the question before the Court was not whether states had the right to segregate, but whether or not individual rights were violated by racial segregation.

Dr. Clark's experiments demonstrated that black children were harmed psychologically by being forced to attend segregated schools.

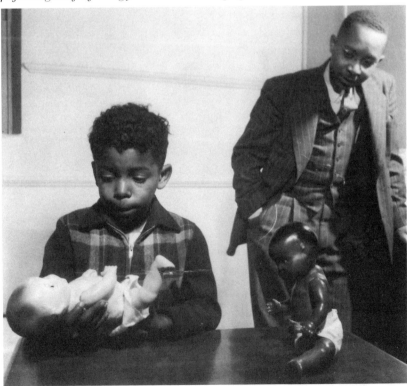

The Fourteenth Amendment, he contended, guaranteed every American "equal protection under the law." He continued:

> The significant factor running through all these arguments is that for some reason, which is still unexplained, Negroes are taken out of the mainstream of American life in these states [that have segregated schools]. There is nothing involved in this case other than race and color. No matter how great anyone becomes, if he happens to have been born a Negro, regardless of his color, he is relegated to that school.[28]

Despite strong, emotional appeals from both sides, the nine justices were unable at first to come to a decision in the *Brown* case and requested that each side return to the Court to reargue the case. They believed it necessary, before rendering a decision, to hear more testimony from both sides of the issue.

Attorney John W. Davis (seen here with Thurgood Marshall), argued in Brown v. Board of Education *that states had a legal right to segregate public schools.*

Marshall argued that the original intent of those who wrote the Fourteenth Amendment was to prohibit all forms of discrimination, including racial segregation.

Returning to the Court

Between Supreme Court appearances in the *Brown* case, a sudden change in the Court took place. Chief Justice Vinson died of a heart attack and President Dwight D. Eisenhower appointed Earl Warren, governor of California, to fill the post. Warren, having had almost no experience as a judge, was somewhat of a judicial unknown. No one knew how he would vote on the issue of desegregation.

Nevertheless, after months of further research by the LDF, legal scholars, and historians, Marshall was satisfied that he had the legal basis that the Court could use to end segregation. The Fourteenth Amendment, Marshall's researchers discovered, was intended by those who wrote it to prohibit discrimination—including racial segregation.

Marshall's closing arguments, explaining his views on the original intent of the Fourteenth Amendment, concluded with a point profoundly affecting the nine justices. Somewhat abandoning his prepared notes, Marshall told the Court that only if someone convincingly argued that blacks were inferior to everyone else could the Court rule in favor of

The Road to a Decision

Every case argued before the U.S. Supreme Court goes through two basic stages—the written brief and the oral argument—before the justices begin to consider their decision. Each side of a case pending before the Court must prepare a written document—the legal brief—which outlines in some detail the factual background of the case and the legal and constitutional points that the attorneys believe should determine the Court's decision.

The oral arguments are the most dramatic part of any hearing by the Supreme Court and the only part of the Court's proceedings that is open to the public. During oral arguments, attorneys for both sides must be prepared to engage in direct discussion with the justices about points needing clarification. Many justices see this aspect of the Court's procedure as the most important, serving to expose the strengths and weaknesses of each case.

Once oral arguments are completed, private deliberations begin. The justices meet in conference once or twice a week, discussing the various cases that they have recently heard. Between conference meetings, each justice studies the cases and the legal questions involved. Once a majority of justices have agreed on a decision, the Chief Justice assigns one member of the Court to write the opinion, which is to be announced during the next public session. Any justices who vote against the majority are allowed to present dissenting opinions at the time that the Court's decision is announced.

---

segregation. Marshall went on to say that only if the Court held that blacks should be kept in conditions very close to slavery could it favor segregation. Marshall concluded, ". . . now is the time, we submit, that this Court should make clear that *that* is not what our Constitution stands for."[29]

The Court's Decision

After months of careful deliberations, the Court's ruling came on May 17, 1954. The Supreme Court chamber was relatively uncrowded when Chief Justice Earl Warren announced that he was about to read the Court's decision in the matter of *Brown v. Board of Education.*

When Warren began reading, it was impossible to tell whether or not the Court had decided in favor of desegregation. The opinion, written in plain, simple language, began with a review of the history of the school cases, the briefs submitted by both sides, the importance of education in the modern world, and the information on the intent of the framers of the Fourteenth Amendment provided to them in reargument.

Then Warren posed the essential question:

> Does segregation of children in public schools solely on the basis of race, even though the physical facilities and other "tangible" factors may be equal, deprive the children of the minority group of equal educational opportunities?

After a short, dramatic pause, he declared:

> We believe, unanimously, that it does. To separate [black children] from others of similar age and qualifications solely because of their race generates a feeling of inferiority as to their status in the community that may affect their hearts and minds in a way unlikely ever to be undone.[30]

Peter Irons, in his history of the Supreme Court, writes that Chief Justice Warren had hoped that a strong, unanimous opinion would prevent resistance to desegregation on the part of Southern states. But, Irons reports, there was widespread dissension among Southern politicians and common citizens:

A mother reads her daughter the news of the Supreme Court's decision in Brown v. Board of Education.

Governors and senators heatedly denounced the ruling. Georgia governor Eugene Talmadge claimed the Court had made the Constitution a "mere scrap of paper." Senator Harry Byrd of Virginia called the decision "the most serious blow that has yet been struck against the rights of the states in a matter vitally affecting their authority and welfare." Governor James Byrnes of South Carolina, a former Supreme Court justice, said he was "shocked" by the Court's action. Senator James Eastland of Mississippi vowed that the South "will not abide by or obey this legislative decision by a political court."[31]

White businessmen, bankers, and lawyers throughout the South formed White Citizens Councils. They worked to bring economic pressure to bear on anyone who even hinted at supporting the Supreme Court's ruling by such tactics as threatening bank foreclosures, canceling insurance policies, and denying credit.

Brown Slowly Opens the Door to Change

Southern states were slow to comply with the Court's decision. In fact, fewer than 2 percent of formerly segregated school districts experienced any desegregation by 1964, and many had to be forced to integrate schools by further legal action.

Despite the Supreme Court's decision, many areas in the South integrated their schools only grudgingly.

Regardless of the slow pace of change brought about by the Court ruling, it served as "a potent catalyst for ambitious social change," according to *The Oxford Companion to the Supreme Court of the United States*.[32] Almost immediately, the Supreme Court cited *Brown* as a precedent in civil rights cases not associated with education. The end of "separate but equal," it seemed, was not limited to the classroom.

In the years that followed the Supreme Court's decision, young activists and demonstrators, inspired by the victory in *Brown*, participated in protest marches, freedom rides, and sit-ins. In the words of essayist Vincent Harding, these young people

> confronted segregation and racism in all of its public bastions . . . in the schools, restaurants, department stores, churches, swimming pools, motels, bus and train depots and toilets. These students, some in their early teens, were about business, the struggle of their people, and they moved to seize and affirm black rights to all public facilities with their own hands. Everywhere they wrote new definitions of black freedom with their blood and scars.[33]

CHAPTER 3
Nonviolence as a Weapon for Civil Rights

Convinced that economic progress would never lead to real equality and that whites would continue to devise ways to evade court-ordered desegregation, the Rev. Dr. Martin Luther King Jr., and others in the civil rights movement decided that direct confrontation—such as protest marches, boycotts, and sit-ins—was needed to stir the conscience of white Americans.

Such a confrontation with the police in Birmingham, Alabama, landed King in jail on April 12, 1963, and provided the stimulus for the "Letter from Birmingham Jail." Written in response to an open letter from local white clergymen critical of King, this document is the clearest and most complete explanation of his motives and of his personal philosophy of nonviolent confrontation.

"Don't Think Like a Slave"

King's father, the Rev. Martin Luther King Sr., taught his son an important lesson—that he could stand up for what he believed in without abandoning his commitment to Christian principles, such as loving one's enemies and turning the other cheek. According to biographer and social scientist, James H. Cone:

> Martin observed that his father did not "turn the other cheek" to the brutalities of the white man but "had begun to strike back." Daddy King did not "bow and smile" when he was insulted, but was always "straightening out the white folks." "When I stand up," he often proclaimed, "I want everyone to know that a *man* is standing there. . . . Nobody can make a slave out of you if you don't think like a slave."[34]

In addition to his father's personal courage and deep Christian faith, King was particularly moved by the assertions in the Declaration of Independence "that all Men are created equal, that they are endowed by their Creator with certain unalienable Rights, that among these are Life, Liberty, and the Pursuit of Happiness."

King grew up firmly believing that America's founders had meant for their words to be broadly applied.

> It [the Declaration] does not say all white men, but it says all men, which includes black men. It does not say all Gentiles, but

it says all men, which includes Jews. It does not say all Protestants, but it says all men, which includes Catholics.[35]

How people who had been denied those rights might gain them was the question. As a student at Morehouse College from 1944 to 1948, King was introduced to the writings of Henry David Thoreau, an American writer and naturalist (one who studies living things in nature by direct observation). Thoreau strongly opposed slavery in America and allowed himself to be imprisoned rather than pay taxes that he believed were funding a federal government that supported slavery. Reading Thoreau's essay "Civil Disobedience," King learned the virtue of refusing to cooperate with unjust laws. Still, he did not see a specific strategy for changing those unjust laws.

Gandhi's Lessons

King found that strategy in 1948 while studying at Crozer Theological Seminary. There he attended a lecture about the work of Mohandas K. "Mahatma" Gandhi (1869–1948). Gandhi, King learned, had led the people of India in their struggle for independence from Great Britain. Their revolution, however, involved no battles and no fighting. Instead, Gandhi had preached nonviolence while at the same time advocating direct confrontation with those in authority. In his view, if a person openly and peacefully defies an unjust law and willingly endures whatever punishment is meted out for that disobedience, a strange thing occurs in the mind of the oppressor. As soon as the injustice comes to light, public opinion, or the oppressor's own conscience, often brings realization of the evil nature of the oppression, and the oppressor then mends his ways.

King was impressed with Gandhi's use of nonviolent noncooperation. In his book *Stride Toward Freedom*, King later wrote:

> Christ furnished the spirit and motivation, while Gandhi furnished the method. . . . Gandhi was probably the first person in history to lift the love ethic of Jesus above the mere interaction between individuals to a powerful and effective social force on a large scale. . . .
>
> I came to feel that this was the only morally and practically sound method open to oppressed people in their struggle for freedom.[36]

King was soon able to put Gandhi's methods to the test. On December 1, 1955, Rosa Parks, a forty-two-year-old African American seamstress, refused to give up her seat to a white person on a segregated city bus in Montgomery, Alabama, and was arrested. Local black leaders called on King to use Parks's arrest as a rallying point to organize and

Mohandas K. Gandhi (1869–1948)

Mohandas Karamchand Gandhi was born into a middle-class family in Poorbandar, India. After a general education in India, he studied law in London. In 1893 he went to South Africa, where he practiced law for seven years. He gave up his practice to fight injustice on behalf of Indian workers—not in the courts but through nonviolent resistance.

Gandhi called his strategy Satyagraha, which means "holding on to the truth" or "truth-force." His methods were so successful in gaining rights for Indians living in South Africa that he felt free to return to India in 1914. His reputation preceded him, and, after a hero's welcome, he found himself the leader of a similar movement in India.

Gandhi was repeatedly jailed in India for his involvement in protest marches, sit-ins, boycotts, and other acts of civil disobedience. His most famous demonstration against the injustice of British colonialism was his "March to the Sea" to protest England's monopoly on the production of salt. Thousands followed him when he walked 200 miles to the seashore, where he made his own salt, thus openly defying British law.

Eventually, Great Britain realized that there was no way to successfully oppose a campaign of this sort and, in 1947, recognized the independence of India. Gandhi, a simple man who never held public office, was nicknamed "Mahatma," which means "having a great soul." He was assassinated in 1948 by a Hindu fanatic who was opposed to his policy of peaceful coexistence with Muslims.

Mohandas Gandhi influenced Martin Luther King Jr.'s philosophy of nonviolent opposition to injustice.

lead a nonviolent campaign to force the city to integrate its buses. At the beginning of the boycott, on Christmas Eve, 1955, King eloquently expressed his nonviolent philosophy:

Hate is too great a burden to bear.

Somehow we must be able to stand up before our most bitter opponents and say: "We shall match your capacity to inflict suffering by our capacity to endure suffering. We will meet your physical force with soul force. Do to us what you will and we will still love you.

We cannot in all good conscience obey your unjust laws and abide by the unjust system, because noncooperation with evil is as much a moral obligation as is cooperation with good, and so throw us in jail and we will still love you.

Bomb our homes and threaten our children . . . and we will still love you.

But be assured that we'll wear you down by our capacity to suffer, and one day we will win our freedom. We will not only win freedom for ourselves, we will so appeal to your heart and conscience that we will win you in the process, and our victory will be a double victory.[37]

Because of the success of the year-long boycott, King rose to the forefront of the fight for civil rights in America. During January 10–11, 1957, after the end of the Montgomery Bus Boycott, the Southern Christian Leadership Conference (SCLC) formed in Atlanta, Georgia, with King as its president. The organization wanted to move beyond what the NAACP was attempting in the courts and carry the success of Montgomery's direct action campaign to other areas of the South.

In Montgomery and in campaigns to follow, King combined Thoreau's ideas on civil disobedience, Gandhi's philosophy of nonviolence, and what he had learned from his father about Christian love and courage into a potent force for change. He called it "Christianity in action."

Putting It All Together in Birmingham

In 1963, King and others in the civil rights movement decided that Birmingham, Alabama, considered by many to be the most segregated city in the South, was the next logical target for their protests. The city's racist mayor and police commissioner, Eugene "Bull" Conner, enthusiastically enforced segregation through local ordinances and a brutal police force. Voting restrictions, arbitrary rulings by city and county officials, and outright intimidation kept most Birmingham blacks compliant.

Arriving on April 3, 1963, King and his associates orchestrated a protest campaign, called "Project C" (for "confrontation"), which they

Eugene "Bull" Connor (right, with glasses) used the Birmingham, Alabama, police force to brutally enforce segregation.

hoped would provoke an angry response from Conner. They were intent upon packing the jails with protestors and, through extensive media coverage, demonstrating to the nation the inherent evil of Jim Crow laws. They began with small groups conducting sit-ins at strictly segregated downtown lunch counters, and Bull Conner's police force soon obliged them by arresting thirty-five protesters—for trespassing.

On Saturday, April 6, protest leaders ordered a march on City Hall. Forty-two were arrested for parading without a permit. Each day, the demonstrations became more widespread. During the week before Easter, King's forces conducted demonstrations at other segregated places in the city—kneel-ins at local churches, sit-ins at the library, and another march on the County Building in support of increased voter registration.

Jail and the Sting of Criticism

On April 10, the city obtained a court order banning further demonstrations. Two days later, on Good Friday, King openly defied the court order by leading a mass march toward the downtown area. King, Ralph Abernathy (treasurer of the SCLC and King's second-in-command), and fifty other marchers were arrested. They were herded into police vans and escorted to jail while television cameras captured the dramatic scene.

The next day, April 13, an open letter from eight white Birmingham clergymen appeared in the *Birmingham News*. In their letter, they criticized the demonstrations, calling them "unwise and untimely." They tried to make an issue of the demonstrations being led by "outsiders" and "extremists,"[38] referring to the fact that King and other SCLC members were not from Birmingham. The clergymen, not critical of the goals of the protesters, but of the protests themselves, continued:

> Just as we formerly pointed out that "hatred and violence have no sanction in our religious and political traditions," we also point out that such actions as incite to hatred and violence, however technically peaceful those actions may be, have not contributed to the resolutions of our local problems. We do not believe that these days of new hope are days when extreme measures are justified in Birmingham.
>
> When rights are consistently denied, a cause should be pressed in the courts and in negotiations among local leaders, and not in the streets. We appeal to both our white and Negro citizenry to observe the principles of law and order and common sense.[39]

Sitting in his jail cell, King read the letter from the clergymen in a newspaper smuggled in by Clarence Jones, an attorney for SCLC. King was deeply disturbed by their statements because these men were not segregationists. They were liberals, many of whom had risked their standing in the community by being openly critical of segregation, and

Martin Luther King Jr. is arrested in Birmingham, Alabama. During his time in jail, King wrote one of his most famous essays, "Letter from Birmingham Jail."

he thought that they should have been his allies. For that reason, their criticism was more painful. Moreover, King believed that his white colleagues were missing the point of desegregation, as biographer James H. Cone explains:

> He was severely critical of white ministers who tolerated segregation in their churches and remained silent about its practice in the society. . . . "I have heard numerous southern religious leaders admonish their worshippers to comply with a desegregation decision because it's the *law*," King said, "but I have longed to hear white ministers declare: 'Follow that decree because integration is morally *right* and because the Negro is your brother.'"[40]

King's Response

Unable to put criticism from his fellow ministers out of his mind, King scribbled a response on the only paper available to him—the margins of

Nonviolent Commitment Card

Every person who wanted to participate in the demonstrations in Birmingham, Alabama, was required to undergo training in nonviolence and to sign a card that read:

> I hereby pledge myself—my person and body—to the nonviolent movement. Therefore I will keep the following ten commandments:
>
> 1. Meditate daily on the teachings and life of Jesus.
> 2. Remember always that the nonviolent movement in Birmingham seeks justice and reconciliation—not victory.
> 3. Walk and talk in the manner of love, for God is love.
> 4. Pray daily to be used by God in order that all men might be free.
> 5. Sacrifice personal wishes in order that all men might be free.
> 6. Observe with both friend and foe the ordinary rules of courtesy.
> 7. Seek to perform regular service for others and for the world.
> 8. Refrain from the violence of fist, tongue, or heart.
> 9. Strive to be in good spiritual and bodily health.
> 10. Follow the directions of the movement and of the captain on a demonstration.
>
> I sign this pledge, having seriously considered what I do and with the determination and will to persevere.

Martin Luther King Jr. is pictured with his wife, Coretta Scott King, in 1964.

the very same April 13 issue of the *Birmingham News*. He filled every blank space in the newspaper—from the margins of the garden club news to spaces around pest control ads.

Still not finished with his response by the following Tuesday, when Jones returned, King borrowed several sheets of note paper and, over the next few days, finished the letter. Jones smuggled the sheets out a few at a time to King's associates.

What resulted when King's scribblings were transcribed was the twenty-page "Letter from Birmingham Jail," dated April 16, 1963. The letter was first published as a pamphlet to be distributed in Southern churches and later was reprinted in national newspapers and magazines. Later that year, it became the centerpiece of King's book *Why We Can't Wait*. Expressing the voice of both a prisoner and a prophet, King's words stirred the conscience of the nation.

In the letter, Dr. King explained as completely as possible why he had come to Birmingham and why he believed that demonstrations were needed there. He spelled out what the goals of the civil rights movement were and why African Americans could not wait any longer for relief from oppression.

King noted that he saw the fight for civil rights in global terms:

> I am in Birmingham because injustice is here. . . . I cannot sit idly by in Atlanta and not be concerned about what happens in Birmingham. Injustice anywhere is a threat to justice everywhere. We

are ... tied in a single garment of destiny. Whatever affects one directly affects all indirectly.[41]

He then turned criticism back on the ministers, saying:

You deplore the demonstrations taking place in Birmingham. But your statement, I am sorry to say, fails to express a similar concern for the conditions that brought about the demonstrations.[42]

Why Direct Action?

King explained to the ministers the reasons for the SCLC's choice of action—why the members chose confrontation rather than negotiation:

Why direct action? Why sit-ins, marches, etc.? Isn't negotiation a better path? You are exactly right in your call for negotiation. Indeed, this is the purpose of direct action. Nonviolent direct action seeks to create such a crisis and establish such creative tension that a community that has constantly refused to negotiate is forced to confront the issue. It seeks so to dramatize the issue that it can no longer be ignored. . . . The purpose of the direct action is to create a situation so crisis-packed that it will inevitably open the door to negotiation.[43]

King was aware of how difficult it was for whites to understand what blacks had to endure. He did, however, manage to paint a vivid picture in his letter of why it was unbearable for African Americans to be told that they should be patient, that change comes slowly—that they would have to wait a little longer. In a sentence containing more than three hundred words, he tried to convey to white readers what black people had endured for generations and therefore why blacks had to demand desegregation *now:*

Perhaps it is easy for those who have never felt the stinging darts of segregation to say, "Wait." But when you have seen vicious mobs lynch your mothers and fathers at will and drown your sisters and brothers at whim; when you have seen hate-filled policemen curse, kick, and even kill your black brothers and sisters; . . . when you suddenly find your tongue twisted and your speech stammering as you seek to explain to your six-year-old daughter why she can't go to the public amusement park that has just been advertised on television, and see tears welling up in her eyes when she is told that Funtown is closed to colored children, and see ominous clouds of inferiority beginning to form in her little mental sky; . . . when you have to concoct an answer for a five-year-old son who is asking: "Daddy, why do white people treat colored people so mean?"; when you are hu-

A group of African American youth set off from the Sixteenth Street Baptist Church in Birmingham, Alabama, on a march for civil rights.

miliated day in and day out by nagging signs reading "white" and "colored"; when your first name becomes "nigger," your middle name becomes "boy" (however old you are) and your last name becomes "John," and your wife and mother are never given the respected title "Mrs."; . . . when you are forever fighting a degenerating sense of "nobodiness"—then you will understand why we find it difficult to wait.[44]

Defying Unjust Laws

Later in his letter, Dr. King addressed the clergymen's concerns that he and his followers had broken laws. In his discussion, he pointed out that not all laws are just or equitable. He noted that although all the acts of Hitler against the Jews in Nazi Germany were legal—done in accordance with laws enacted by the nation's government—they were certainly not just. King quoted Saint Thomas Aquinas's statement that "an unjust law is no law at all" and went on to say:

> Any law that uplifts human personality is just. Any law that degrades human personality is unjust. All segregation statutes are unjust because segregation distorts the soul and damages the personality. It gives the segregator a false sense of superiority and the segregated a false sense of inferiority.[45]

Demonstrators show their adherence to King's philosophy of nonviolence by gathering peacefully and praying outside a municipal building in Birmingham.

In later paragraphs, Dr. King expressed his disappointment with white moderates. Their unwillingness to stand up publicly for what they knew to be right, he said, was perhaps more damaging to the cause of equality than the activities of extremists in the Ku Klux Klan and White Citizens' Councils. He also criticized the clergymen's charge that nonviolent demonstrations by blacks had led to violence. He compared that charge to telling someone who has been robbed that it was his or her wealth that brought on the theft.

Extremists?

Finally, he addressed the clergymen's charge that the SCLC's activities in Birmingham had been extreme, saying:

> But though I was initially disappointed at being categorized as an extremist, as I continued to think about the matter I gradually gained a measure of satisfaction from the label. Was not Jesus an extremist for love: "Love your enemies, bless them that curse you, do good to them that hate you, and pray for them which despitefully use you, and persecute you." . . . Was not Amos an extremist for justice. . . . Was not Paul an extremist for the Christian gospel. . . . Was not Martin Luther an extremist. . . . And Abraham Lincoln: "This nation cannot survive half slave and half free." And Thomas Jefferson: "We hold these truths to be self-evident, that all men are created equal. . . ." So the ques-

tion is not whether we will be extremists, but what kind of extremists we will be. Will we be extremists for the preservation of injustice or for the extension of justice?[46]

The Birmingham Children's Protest

When King's letter became public, it was initially overshadowed by other events taking place in Birmingham. While he was still in jail, other members of SCLC carried out a children's protest. James Bevel, a veteran of other civil rights demonstrations, had convinced Dr. King and others in the SCLC that they should schedule a "D" Day, in which thousands of protesters, mostly students, would flood the streets. This act, they hoped, would goad Bull Conner into an extreme response. Extensive media coverage of schoolchildren being herded to jail, Bevel thought, would clearly demonstrate to the country the true nature of Birmingham's race policies.

On May 2, wave after wave of young people gathered at the Sixteenth Street Baptist Church to begin their demonstrations. True to form, Bull Conner arrested more than a thousand of them, but day after day, they came. School principals tried to restrain their students by threatening expulsion or, in one case, by locking the gates to keep them in. Students would not be denied, however, and climbed the gates to join the protests.

A Horrified Nation Watches

At the height of the campaign, there were 2,500 demonstrators in Birmingham jails, most of them students. Under such pressure and national

Birmingham firefighters prepare to use fire hoses to disperse a group of civil rights demonstrators.

scrutiny, Conner finally broke down and ordered his officers to use force to disperse the crowds—police dogs, nightsticks, and fire hoses with enough water pressure to rip the bark off trees.

Worldwide, the front pages of newspapers and television news programs carried images of "prostrate women, and policemen bending over them with raised clubs; of children marching up to the bared fangs of police dogs; of the terrible force of pressure hoses sweeping bodies into the streets."[47]

The effect of such scenes on African Americans around the country was phenomenal. Seeing innocent children taking the brunt of Southern anger forced blacks who had previously been reluctant to participate to join the movement. People of all ages and occupations joined protest marches throughout the South.

Victory in Birmingham

The national outcry in response to Birmingham's handling of the demonstrations forced city officials to consider the effect that such publicity was having on their city's reputation. They opened negotiations with protesters, and on Friday, May 10, an agreement was announced. Lunch counters, restrooms, fitting rooms, and drinking fountains would be desegregated. A nondiscriminatory hiring policy would be put into effect so that blacks could be employed in jobs previously denied to them.

The Birmingham campaign became a great victory for the civil rights movement. It was a turning point in African Americans' struggle for equality and fair treatment. Some question the actual role that King's letter played in galvanizing the civil rights movement even while acknowledging its moral power. According to historian Taylor Branch:

> In hindsight, it appeared that King had rescued the beleaguered Birmingham movement with his pen, but the reverse was true: unexpected miracles of the Birmingham movement later transformed King's letter from a silent cry of desperate hope to a famous pronouncement of moral triumph.[48]

But as the document that laid out the rationale for nonviolent protest used by King, his "Letter from Birmingham Jail" has come to be seen as one of the most significant documents in the history of the civil rights movement.

Moved by the events in Birmingham and convinced that the time had come for the federal government to right old wrongs, President John F. Kennedy addressed the nation on June 11, 1963. In his speech, he called for Congress to commit itself to the removal of racial distinctions from American life and law.

After witnessing the events in Birmingham, President John F. Kennedy called for an end to racial segregation in the United States.

To the American people, he said:

If an American, because his skin is dark, cannot eat lunch in a restaurant open to the public; if he cannot send his children to the best public school available; if he cannot vote for the public officials who represent him; if, in short, he cannot enjoy the full and free life which all of us want, then who among us would be content to have the color of his skin changed and stand in his place? Who among us would then be content with the counsels of patience and delay?

This nation, for all its hopes and all its boasts, will not be fully free until all its citizens are free.

We preach freedom around the world, and we mean it, and we cherish our freedom here at home; but are we to say to the world, and much more importantly to each other, that this is a land of the free, except for the Negroes; that we have no second-class citizens, except Negroes; that we have no class or caste system, no ghettos, no master race, except with respect to Negroes?[49]

The Legacy of King's Letter

The success of the Birmingham campaign and the distribution of more than one million copies of "Letter from Birmingham Jail," mainly in Northern churches, led the National Council of Churches (NCC) to urge its thirty-one member denominations to begin nationwide demonstrations against racial discrimination. Protestant denominations also set up groups called Commissions on Race to study the issue and determine what they could do to help.

In late August 1963, white churches throughout the North contributed financially to and participated in the historic March on Washington, which King and others had been planning. Standing proudly on the steps of the Lincoln Memorial on August 28, a hot summer day, representatives of the NCC, along with the rest of the world, listened as King spoke to the nation about his dreams for America in a speech that has come to be known by the repeated phrase "I Have a Dream."

King did not live to see the realization of his dreams. He was assassinated in Memphis, Tennessee, on April 4, 1968, while conducting another nonviolent protest campaign. More than eighteen years later, on November 2, 1986, President Ronald Reagan issued the proclamation establishing Martin Luther King Day:

> Dr. King's was truly a prophetic voice that reached out over the chasms of hostility, prejudice, ignorance, and fear to touch the conscience of America. He challenged us to make real the promise of America as a land of freedom, equality, opportunity, and brotherhood.
>
> The majesty of his message, the dignity of his bearing, and the righteousness of his cause are a lasting legacy. In a few short years he changed America for all time. He made it possible for our nation to move closer to the ideals set forth in our Declaration of Independence: that all people are created equal and are endowed with inalienable rights that government has the duty to respect and protect.[50]

Chapter 4
The Fight for a Political Voice

"The right of citizens of the United States to vote shall not be denied or abridged by the United States or by any State on account of race, color, or previous condition of servitude."[51] These words from the Fifteenth Amendment to the United States Constitution, ratified on February 8, 1870, seem simple and were supposed to guarantee voting rights for former slaves, but they did not.

It was this right to vote that Fannie Lou Hamer and many others fought very hard to obtain. Hamer, a poor, uneducated sharecropper from the Mississippi Delta, lived at first like many other rural Southern blacks—at the whim of Southern landowners for her meager livelihood and, since she had no access to the polls, seemingly without any power to change white-dominated society. The arrival in Mississippi of civil rights activists helped open the door to that power.

In the summer of 1962, black citizens from the Ruleville, Mississippi, area heard representatives from several civil rights organizations speak about the importance of voting. The meeting, sponsored by the Council of Federated Organizations (COFO), convinced Hamer and others that only through voting would they be able to bring change to the Delta. COFO, a civil rights group established in 1961 to coordinate the activities of the NAACP and other civil rights organizations in the South, encouraged local

Fannie Lou Hamer worked for many years so African Americans in Mississippi could exercise their right to vote.

citizens in rural areas to exercise their constitutional rights. Inspired by what they heard, Hamer and others volunteered to attempt to register, despite the very real danger of violence on the part of white Southerners intent upon preventing such an occurrence.

Her courage and determination, along with that of many others, eventually led the way to new federal legislation against practices that limited voting by blacks. Hamer's story, about what happened to her when she tried to register to vote, shocked the nation and helped stir lawmakers to action. Hamer, however, was not the first African American to see voting as a means to achieving the equality promised by the Fourteenth Amendment.

Early Supporters of Black Voting Rights

During the mid-1860s, shortly before passage of the Fourteenth Amendment, various individuals and organizations called for African American suffrage (the right to vote). In 1864, more than one hundred African American men met in Syracuse, New York, for the National Convention of Colored Citizens. Aware that the end of the Civil War was near, they proposed a postwar political agenda for America's blacks, which included securing voting rights. Among those in attendance was Frederick Douglass, the nation's most prominent abolitionist.

Although some present at the convention thought that blacks should separate themselves from white society, most believed that the end of the war would bring full acceptance of African Americans into mainstream American society. To that end, the convention founded the National Equal Rights League, with lawyer John Mercer Langston as president. Langston, in his "Address to the Colored People of the United States," encouraged blacks to form local units of the Equal Rights League to fight for their rights.

Just after the war, in 1866, Radical Republicans, a group of members of Congress who demanded sweeping changes in the former Confederacy, held a meeting in Philadelphia to call for increased black civil rights. Douglass, attending as a delegate from New York, spoke out for black suffrage.

With passage of the Civil Rights Act of 1866 and the Fourteenth Amendment in 1867, Congress conferred on African Americans all civil rights enjoyed by whites, except the vote. Voting at first was considered a privilege rather than a right and was left up to the states to control, but the Fifteenth Amendment, ratified in 1870, guaranteed the right of African Americans to vote.

Early in the twentieth century, years after passage of the Fifteenth Amendment and the end of Reconstruction, blacks still did not have the vote in many areas of the country. During that time, there were two voices competing to represent African Americans in the United States—those of Booker T. Washington and W. E. B. Du Bois. Washington favored postponing demands by blacks for voting and other political rights in exchange for vocational education. Du Bois, on the other hand, believed that the right to vote was one of America's basic civil rights and that it was essential to democracy. Without it, he thought a person had no voice, no opinion, in the decisions of the state. In other words, a person who did not have the vote was not a true citizen of the nation.

In 1903, Du Bois published *The Souls of Black Folk*, in which he criticized Washington's strategy and attacked the disfranchisement (denial of rights) and segregation still rampant in the South. He urged black leaders to demand every right pledged in the Declaration of Independence and the Constitution. Two years later, in 1905, Du Bois met with some thirty other black intellectuals at Niagara Falls, New York, to address the problem of the nation's policy toward African Americans and to demand the vote for black men. (At the time, no woman of any race could vote.)

The following year, the Niagara Movement, as it was called, issued a scalding manifesto to the nation, written by Du Bois—a list of demands, specifically including voting rights, which were essential to all other rights:

> [We] would vote; with the right to vote goes everything: Freedom, manhood, the honor of our wives, the chastity [purity] of your daughters, the right to work, and the chance to rise, and let no man listen to those who deny this.
>
> We want full manhood suffrage, and we want it now, henceforth and forever.[52]

W. E. B. Du Bois struggled to secure voting rights for African Americans.

Many organizers of the Niagara Movement, including W. E. B. Du Bois, later founded the National Association for the Advancement of Colored People (NAACP), an interracial group whose mission was to fight for equal rights for African Americans. Du Bois served as director of research for the association and editor of its journal, *The Crisis*. The journal, which stood for "the highest ideals of American democracy, and for reasonable but earnest and persistent attempts to gain these rights and realize these ideals,"[53] published countless articles calling for equal voting rights throughout the country for people of all races.

When in 1917 the United States became involved in World War I, thousands of black soldiers joined the fight. In 1919, when American troops, both black and white, returned from the war, Du Bois, in *The Crisis*, put into words the feelings of black soldiers about to return to America's Jim Crow society:

> We are returning from war! For bleeding France, . . . we fought gladly and to the last drop of blood; for America and her highest ideals, we fought in far-off hope; for the dominant southern oligarchy [Southern Democrats] entrenched in Washington, we fought in bitter resignation. For the America that represents and gloats in lynching, disfranchisement, caste [class separated by birth], brutality and devilish insult—for this, in the hateful upturning and mixing of things, we were forced by vindictive [vengeful] fate to fight, also.
>
> But today we return! We stand again to look America squarely in the face. We sing: This country of ours, despite all its better souls have done and dreamed, is yet a shameful land.
>
> It disfranchises its own citizens.
>
> Disfranchisement is the deliberate theft and robbery of the only protection of poor against rich and black against white. The land that disfranchises its citizens and calls itself a democracy lies and knows it lies.[54]

Change Comes Slowly to the Mississippi Delta

DuBois and his colleagues failed in their efforts to secure voting rights following World War I. In fact, not much changed in the lives of black farm workers in the Mississippi Delta throughout the 1940s and 1950s. By the 1960s, though, new ideas came to even the remotest rural areas of Mississippi. Organizations such as the Southern Christian Leadership Conference (SCLC) and the Student Nonviolent Coordinating Committee (SNCC) sent volunteers to the South to recruit black voters. SCLC, formed by the Rev. Dr. Martin Luther King Jr., and Ralph Abernathy after the Montgomery Bus Boycott, consisted primarily of black ministers and was committed to King's goal of achieving an integrated and racially just society through nonviolent means.

SNCC (pronounced "Snick") was originally composed of black and white college students from across the country who wanted to protest the social system of the South through lunch counter sit-ins, boycotts, and lawsuits. Organized as a decentralized, community-based movement, SNCC was, in many ways, the heart of the civil rights movement in the South. After its initial involvement with sit-ins and other forms of protest, SNCC members came to see that voter registration in the predominantly black areas of the South would bring about a more lasting improvement in the lives of African Americans. In 1960, SNCC began a series of voter registration meetings in Mississippi to accomplish that goal.

Hamer began crusading for voting rights after a SNCC meeting held in Ruleville, Mississippi.

One such meeting was held on August 27, 1962, at the Williams Chapel Missionary Baptist Church, in Ruleville, Mississippi. Fannie Lou Hamer, along with other concerned black citizens of the area, attended to learn what voting was all about and how it could help rural blacks in Mississippi. James Bevel, a young minister with SCLC, opened the program, followed by SNCC executive director James Forman. Hamer later recalled:

> He [Forman] told us . . . we could vote out people and . . . talked about . . . hateful policemen and how they had been elected and if we had a chance to vote . . . that we wouldn't allow these people to be in office because we could vote them out.[55]

Also at the meeting were two other SNCC members, Reginald Robinson and Robert Parris Moses. Moses would later become head of SNCC's Mississippi program and director of COFO operations in the state. As one of the most important African American leaders in the movement, Moses contributed significantly to its success.

Robert Parris Moses

Robert Parris "Bob" Moses had received his master's degree in philosophy from Harvard University in 1957 and had been accepted into a doctoral

Robert Parris Moses (1935–) and Freedom Summer in Mississippi

Robert Moses, the soft-spoken but dedicated leader of SNCC's Mississippi campaign, was born in New York City and educated at Hamilton College and Harvard University. He gave up a promising career in mathematics to join the civil rights movement.

Joining the effort to register black voters in Mississippi, he soon emerged as a leader, organizing the grass-roots movement. After a couple of years in the Delta participating in sit-ins and voter registration drives, he convinced his fellow activisists of the need for a larger campaign against Mississippi's voter registration system, which was designed to exclude blacks from the electoral process.

In the summer of 1964—Freedom Summer—at the urging of SNCC, nearly one thousand volunteers—mostly black and white students from Northern colleges—came to Mississippi to staff "freedom schools" that would teach African Americans how to register to vote. They endured death threats, bombings, and police harassment, but their crusade had a significant impact on the state.

---

program in mathematics at Harvard when he became interested in the civil rights movement. His study of philosophy, and particularly the works of French writer Albert Camus, awakened that interest. Camus, in his book *The Rebel* (published in 1951), rejected revolution as an effective method for change and instead chose what he called "rebellion."

To Camus, rebellion was "a continuing personal assertion of conscience and freedom in the face of whatever . . . threatens freedom and life." In other words, a rebel stands firm in his or her beliefs and is willing to endure hardships without retaliation—without being "either victim or executioner."[56] To Moses, the philosophy of nonviolence central to the civil rights movement and Camus's idea of rebellion fit together perfectly.

Moses went to Mississippi in 1960 to volunteer his services in SCLC's voter registration project. Once there, he found that he had more in common with members of SNCC than with those in SCLC, although both organizations shared his idea of rebellion. According to biographer Eric R. Burner:

> Even in the pre-SNCC civil rights movement, the act of rebellion was both a means to freedom and a personal enactment of freedom by each participant: leaders, footsore black domestics, politely defiant students. And that empowerment of individu-

als was what Robert Moses would come to envision for black Mississippi.[57]

In Mississippi, Moses visited Amzie Moore, a longtime veteran in the state's civil rights struggle. Throughout the 1950s, Moore had worked for voter registration projects as head of the local chapter of the NAACP, but with limited success. Moore convinced Moses that direct action, such as sit-ins and other demonstrations employed elsewhere in the South, was too dangerous in the Delta region of the state and that, in Mississippi, voter registration was itself an act of confrontation.

During his four-year stay in Mississippi, Moses recruited new voters, taught them how to fill out registration forms and how to be ready to answer questions county registrars would pose, and drove them to county courthouses to register. It was to recruit new voters that Moses visited Ruleville, Mississippi, in August 1962.

Standing Up to Be Counted

When Moses asked the gathering for volunteers, Hamer, along with seventeen of her neighbors, said that they would go to register to vote. Later, Hamer would characterize her decision as being made on the spur of the moment. As she put it:

> When they asked for those to raise their hands who'd go down to the courthouse the next day, I raised mine. Had it up as high as I could get it. I guess if I'd had any sense I'd a been a little scared. The only thing they could do to me was kill me and it seemed like they'd been trying to do that a little bit at a time ever since I could remember.[58]

However, according to Hamer's biographer Chana Kai Lee:

> Hamer's decision to get involved in voter registration work was not, as

Fannie Lou Hamer participates in a civil rights demonstration in Hattiesburg, Mississippi.

she put it, a "bolt out of the blue." The vote symbolized hope and empowerment for the individual. She had reflected and dreamed about its transformative potential. It represented a way out of a seemingly hopeless and permanent situation. It was a concrete response to the perpetual injustice that filled the lives

Mississippi Voter Registration Procedure

In order to register to vote in the state of Mississippi in 1962, a person had to follow certain procedures. First, the applicant had to go to the office of the Registrar, usually in the county courthouse, where he or she would be given an application blank to fill out. The applicant had to complete this form perfectly, "in his own handwriting in the presence of the registrar and without assistance or suggestion of any person or memorandum."

The first seventeen questions required detailed information about the applicant's name, residence, occupation, employer, and criminal record. Question Number Eighteen read, "Write and copy in the space below, Section ___ of the Constitution of Mississippi: (Instructions to Registrar: You will designate the Section of the Constitution and point out same to applicant)." Black applicants knew that, when copying the assigned section, even one undotted *i* or one uncrossed *t* would be enough to disqualify them.

Question Number Nineteen demanded that the applicant write "a reasonable interpretation [the meaning] of the Section of the Constitution of Mississippi which you have just copied." It was up to the Registrar to assess the adequacy of the answer. Finally, Question Number Twenty stated, "Write in the space below a statement setting forth your understanding of the duties and obligations of citizenship under a constitutional form of government."

Below the questions was a lengthy oath that had to be sworn to orally, followed by a place for the applicant to sign. At the bottom of the form were the following questions for the Registrar: "Is applicant of good moral character?"; "If not, why?"; "Does applicant qualify?"

After the form was completed, the applicant had to wait thirty days for a ruling on his or her application. During this time, his or her name and address were published in the local newspaper twice. Finally, after the waiting period, the applicant returned to the courthouse to find out whether or not he or she had passed. If so, the applicant signed the book and became a registered voter. If not, the test could be retaken.

of the southern poor. Voting was a practical answer for a very practical, no-nonsense woman who was exceedingly impatient for something better.[59]

Treated with contempt and disrespect by county officials on her first registration attempt, Hamer failed to qualify. She returned in December and succeeded on her second attempt to pass the state's literacy test. She became a registered voter and subsequently joined SNCC's efforts to recruit other voters.

SNCC's leaders encouraged Hamer to increase her involvement and leadership in the effort to gain political power for blacks in Mississippi. Aware that having the vote, although important, was of little value when the only candidates for public office were white segregationists, Hamer, encouraged by SNCC allies, decided that the next logical step for her was to become an alternative candidate for Congress in the state's Second District. According to biographer Lee:

> At a campaign meeting in Clarksdale on April 1 [1964], Hamer told a group of supporters that she wanted to "go to Washington to right the wrongs" committed by the twenty-three-year incumbent, [Jamie] Whitten. Her campaign slogan was "justice today for all Mississippians."[60]

Hamer, who stated that she was running for office partly to show other African Americans that it was possible, came in a distant second to Whitten in the primary election but further opened the door for other political activists in the state.

The Road to the Democratic National Convention

Part of the campaign strategy of Hamer in the congressional election had been telling voters and the press of her experiences as a poor black woman trying to exercise her political rights in Mississippi. She recounted episodes of discrimination from her childhood, told about unfair practices that she had witnessed in the voter registration process, and recounted the story of the ordeal that she went through when in June 1963, she and seven other SNCC workers were arrested on trumped-up charges and jailed in Winona, Mississippi, where they were brutally beaten by their jailers.

The effort to place a black candidate for Congress on the ballot was just one of many tactics aimed at increasing the electoral strength of blacks. In 1964, a national presidential election year, blacks in Mississippi decided to challenge the right of the state's all-white Democratic delegation to represent Mississippi voters at the Democratic National Convention. Because few blacks in Mississippi had a voice in the selection of delegates at the state convention, three hundred people, including Fannie Lou Hamer, met in Jackson on April 26 to form the Mississippi Freedom Democratic Party (MFDP) and to elect their own representatives to the national convention. Hamer was chosen as one of those representatives.

Once in Atlantic City, the site of the convention, both Mississippi delegations claimed to represent the people of the state. Since a formal challenge for the state's seats was made, it was up to the Democratic Party's Credentials Committee to decide the issue. Hearings were held on August 22, 1964, before a 108-member panel. Various speakers addressed the group on behalf of the MFDP, including the Rev. Dr. Martin Luther King Jr., but the speeches of all the others were overshadowed by the simple, direct, emotional words of Fannie Lou Hamer.

I Question America

Millions of Americans watched on national television while she spoke. Virtually unknown outside Mississippi before these hearings, this short,

Members of the MFDP quietly protest next to the Mississippi delegation's area at the 1964 Democratic National Convention in Atlantic City, New Jersey.

stocky woman, who had inspired countless young African Americans to join the fight in her home state, slowly recounted to the committee, and to the nation, her experiences at the hands of white Southerners. It became clear that she was "the real thing." According to historian John Dittmer:

> The several million Americans watching the proceedings on television had known little if anything about Mrs. Hamer, but as she graphically described her life, her eviction from the plantation when she registered to vote, and, most dramatically, her beating in the Winona jail, it soon became apparent that hers was an authentic voice describing simply yet powerfully the reality of life in the closed society [of Mississippi].[61]

During the eight minutes allotted to her, Mrs. Hamer spoke without prepared notes about her experience in the Winona jail:

> [A] State Highway Patrolman . . . said, "We are going to make you wish you was dead."
>
> I was carried . . . into another cell where they had two Negro prisoners. The State Highway Patrolman ordered the first Negro prisoner to take the blackjack. [He] ordered me . . . to lay down on a bunk bed on my face. . . . I was beat by the first Negro until he was exhausted. . . . The second Negro began to beat [me] and I began to work my feet, and the State Highway Patrolman ordered the first Negro . . . to set on my feet to keep me from working my feet. I began to scream and one white man got up and began to beat me in my head and tell me to hush.

After a short pause, she concluded, speaking directly to committee members. With tears in her eyes, she indicted the South for its racial policy and the entire country for its lack of action on the race question:

> All of this is on account we want to register, to become first-class citizens, and if the Freedom Democratic Party is not seated now, I question America, is this America, the land of the free and the home of the brave where we have to sleep with our telephones off the hooks because our lives be threatened daily, because we want to live as decent human beings, in America?[62]

After she thanked the committee, someone removed her microphone. She wiped tears from her eyes, gathered her purse, and left the witness table.

Hamer's speech before the Democratic Party's credentials committee moved the entire nation.

Speaking later to a reporter from *Jet* magazine, she said, "I felt just like I was telling it from the mountain. That's why I like that song 'Go Tell It on the Mountain.' I feel like I'm talking to the world."[63]

Immediate Reactions

When her testimony began, Hamer was speaking not only to members of the committee but also to a nationwide television audience. By the time she finished, though, the committee members were the only ones listening. About halfway through her eight-minute address, President Lyndon B. Johnson, who had been watching the proceedings, called an emergency press conference, thereby preempting network coverage of Hamer's testimony.

Johnson was actually in favor of increased political power for blacks, but he was running for reelection in 1964 and was anxious not to create a rift among Democrats that could cost him the election or alienate members of Congress. Hamer's testimony was so real, so powerful, and so damning that he also feared that white Southern delegates to the convention would be offended and either not vote for his nomination or walk out of the convention altogether.

Despite the president's efforts to keep Hamer's comments off the air, the nation was able to hear her entire testimony later that night on the evening news. National exposure brought a mood of euphoria to the MFDP delegates at their Atlantic City headquarters. Hundreds of telegrams poured in from supporters and well-wishers across the country.

Tracy Sugarman, a civil rights activist and author, described the effect that Mrs. Hamer's words had on the national television audience:

> [The] searing testimony of Fannie Lou Hamer . . . became the exciting story of the convention. Throughout the nation, men and women sat riveted to their television screens, compelled and deeply moved by the testimony of this untutored woman

from the Delta. The recital of her sadistic beating by Mississippi police tore the veil that conceals the brutality of life in the South. For many Americans it was their first appalling confrontation with the calculated savagery of white supremacy.[64]

Not for "No Two Seats"

Hamer's story, along with other testimony about the way that the regular Mississippi delegation had been chosen, convinced the Credentials Committee to offer a compromise. On August 25, trying to please everyone involved and avoid more discord at the convention, the committee decided to allow the regular Mississippi delegation to be seated but offered the MFDP two at-large delegate seats (seats representing the whole state rather than a specific district). The decision about who would occupy those seats, however, would not be made by the MFDP.

That evening, MFDP delegates had an emotional discussion. Black leaders urged MFDP delegates to accept the compromise, but Hamer summed up the delegates' feelings about the offer, saying:

New Jersey State Police set up a blockade in an attempt to keep members of the MFDP from entering the convention hall.

The offer of two votes for two named people was exactly the kind of offer that might be expected from Southern whites, and was exactly the reason the Freedom Party was fighting for justice in Mississippi.

A little later in the meeting, she declared emphatically, "We didn't come all this way for no two seats when all of us is tired!"[65] Neither the MFDP nor the regular Mississippi delegation liked the compromise, but in the end, both groups agreed to it.

Legacy of the MFDP Challenge

Although the MFDP did not secure the convention seats that they had sought, they did accomplish one significant thing at the convention. The committee vowed that, in future conventions, no delegations would be seated that had not been chosen by a vote open to all the party's registered voters. This was the first time that a national political party had made such a pledge. The MFDP challenge, and especially Hamer's testimony, opened the way for increased political participation for minorities. Thanks in large measure to her own efforts in 1964, Hamer was seated as a member of Mississippi's delegation to the 1968 Democratic National Convention.

Just nine years later, Fannie Lou Hamer died after a lengthy fight with breast cancer, diabetes, and hypertension. At her funeral, Andrew Young, at that time U.S. Representative to the United Nations, delivered her eulogy. Of Hamer's legacy, Young told the assembled throng of civil rights activists:

> [She] literally, along with many of you, shook the foundations of this nation, and everything I learned about preaching, politics, life and death, I learned in your midst. The many people who are now elected officials would not be where they are had we not stood up then. And there was not a one of those that was not influenced and inspired by the spirit of this one woman, Mrs. Hamer.[66]

Also speaking in her memory was Hodding Carter III, a white Mississippian, a newspaperman, a longtime supporter of the civil rights movement, and, at the time, the Assistant Secretary of State. In his oration, he expressed what many whites in the state, looking back on the "closed society" of the past, wished that they could say to Mrs. Hamer:

> I think history will say that among those who were freed more totally and earlier by her were white Mississippians who were finally freed, if they had the will to be free, from themselves, from their history, from their racism, from their past. And I

Andrew Young (1932–)

Trained as a Congregationalist minister, Andrew Young joined the Southern Christian Leadership Conference (SCLC) in 1960 and soon became one of the Rev. Dr. Martin Luther King Jr.'s inner circle of associates. He served as the executive director of SCLC from 1964 to 1970 and, in 1973, became the first African American elected to represent Georgia in the House of Representatives since Reconstruction.

In 1977 Young left Congress to accept President Jimmy Carter's appointment as U.S. Representative to the United Nations. In 1981 he was elected mayor of Atlanta, Georgia, a position that he held until 1989. Young, whose autobiography, *An Easy Burden*, recounts his experiences in the civil rights movement, continues to be a moderate voice for the African American community.

Andrew Young, who has served in the U.S. Congress and as the American ambassador to the UN and later as mayor of Atlanta, Georgia, was influenced by Hamer's actions.

know that there's no way for us who have been freed to adequately thank those who freed us except to try also to continue the work which Mrs. Hamer and so many of you began, are continuing and will continue in the future. I'm glad I had the chance to be here. I'm gladder yet that I can say that I am from here because of Mrs. Hamer and because of many of you.[67]

CHAPTER 5
Rejection of Integration

While the majority of civil rights activists were convinced that equality and integration were necessarily linked, some African Americans believed that they could never achieve any degree of equality in an integrated America. They thought that African Americans should be self-sufficient, depending on no one but themselves. They should not wait for the nation's white-dominated social and political system to give them their rights. They should demand them—take them—by whatever means necessary.

Unlike the mainstream civil rights movement, which originally sought peaceful integration with white society for poor Southern blacks, this radical, militant philosophy was more likely to be held by Northern urban ghetto dwellers. Black nationalism, as it was called, was frightening to most white Americans, as well as to many black moderates, because of its militancy and seeming advocacy of violence.

Malcolm X was a vocal advocate for black nationalism.

Malcolm X, the most prominent spokesman for black nationalism, was often critical of the white power structure, of discrimination against black workers, and of the slow pace of progress achieved by the efforts of more moderate black leaders. Malcolm X, however, was not the first African American to reject integration.

The Origins of Black Nationalism

Even before the Civil War put an end to slavery in the United States, there were blacks who dreamed of returning to Africa to establish

Marcus Garvey (1887–1940)

Born in St. Ann's Bay, Jamaica, Marcus Garvey immigrated to the United States in 1916, bringing his black nationalist ideas with him. His organization, the Universal Negro Improvement Association (UNIA), tried to instill pride in black people and in their African heritage.

Marcus Garvey aimed his message of racial and cultural pride at the urban poor.

Other newly formed organizations, the National Urban League (NUL) and the National Association for the Advancement of Colored People (NAACP), had aimed their messages mostly at middle-class blacks, virtually ignoring the working class. Focusing his message of racial and cultural pride at the urban poor, Garvey was able, through his speeches and his newspaper, *The Negro World*, to gain a substantial following by 1919. By the mid-1920s, Garvey's movement had an estimated million followers.

Despite the failure of Garvey's plan to emigrate to Africa with his followers, he is remembered as the first black person in the history of the United States to lead a mass movement of black people. His stirring message of black self-sufficiency and pride influenced a generation.

an independent nation. In the mid-1850s, Martin Delany, a freeborn black doctor, proposed transporting African Americans to what is now Nigeria. His plans for black emigration to Africa foundered when the Civil War erupted.

The abolition of slavery, brought about by the victory of the North in the Civil War, raised hopes among black Americans that equality with whites was at hand. As a result, interest in black nationalism waned. By 1877, however, Reconstruction ended, and blacks saw their newly granted rights slowly being eroded. This change brought about a resurgence of nationalist spirit. Once again, Martin Delany led the way. This time, he formed the Liberian Exodus Joint Stock Steamship Company to transport African Americans to Africa. Financial trouble soon ended this venture, however.

Black Nationalism into the Twentieth Century

The collapse of Delany's plan did not end interest in a return to Africa, however. The most outspoken advocate of emigration in the last years of the nineteenth century was a bishop in the African Methodist Episcopal (AME) Church, Henry McNeal Turner. Turner believed God intended for Africans to be enslaved in America and then freed to return to Africa, bringing Christianity with them to redeem and civilize the continent. In his view, God had intended for whites to join in the effort, but they had foiled the plan by keeping American blacks uneducated and poor. Most other black leaders, including fellow ministers, opposed Turner's ideas, and his calls for a return to Africa were largely ignored.

Other black nationalists had more success. In 1916, a Jamaican named Marcus Garvey came to the United States and formed the American branch of the Universal Negro Improvement Association (UNIA). Garvey was convinced that black people would never be accepted, much less respected, until they had their own independent nation in Africa.

In 1920, Garvey organized an International Convention of Negro Peoples of the World, and twenty-five thousand delegates from twenty-five countries came to New York City to attend. Garvey was certain that blacks should—and would—rule Africa. He proclaimed to those attending the convention:

> Wake up Ethiopia! Wake up Africa! Let us work towards the one glorious end of a free, redeemed and mighty nation. Let Africa be a bright star among the constellation of nations. A race without authority is a race without respect.[68]

Critical of integration, Garvey thought that any black organization that depended upon whites for financial help (as the NAACP did at the time) was hindering the progress of blacks.

Earlier, when his nationalist ideas had begun to catch on in the United States, Garvey had formed the Black Star Steamship Corporation as part of a larger plan to establish an independent black economy. Raising money through the sale of stock, he had purchased three ships. But financial problems sent his corporation into bankruptcy by the end of 1920. By 1921, Garvey was in jail for mail fraud, and in 1927, he was deported to Jamaica.

The failure of Garvey's efforts did not end interest on the part of many blacks in economic and political separatism. Black nationalism combined with the Islamic faith in Chicago in 1925, when Noble Drew

Ali (born Timothy Drew) established the Moorish Science Temple of America. Ali rejected Christianity and white society, encouraging his followers to change their surnames, which often had been given to their American ancestors by slaveowners, to Islamic ones in recognition of the faith practiced by many of their African ancestors. Ali believed that African Americans should be economically self-sufficient and follow the religion of Islam. When filling out federal, state, and local forms, he advised, blacks should call themselves Moors.

The Nation of Islam

The Moorish Science Temple laid the groundwork for the most influential black nationalist organization in American history. Ali died mysteriously in 1929, and Wallace D. Fard assumed leadership of the movement, founding the Nation of Islam. When Fard disappeared in 1933, his disciple, Elijah Poole (renamed Elijah Muhammad by Fard), told his followers that Fard was actually Allah (the Muslim name for God), that he had come to North America in person to teach there, and that he had anointed Muhammad as his Messenger.

The Nation of Islam rejected Christianity because it was the religion of white people. Elijah Muhammad preached that whites were evil and therefore were excluded from participation in Islam and from entrance into heaven. According to social scientist and author James H. Cone, one of the Nation of Islam's defining doctrines was that whites were

Nation of Islam leader Elijah Muhammad taught that blacks needed to separate themselves from white society.

snakes who were incapable of doing right, devils who would soon be destroyed by God's righteous judgement. White people, therefore, were identified as the sole cause of black oppression. . . . The logical extension of this doctrine is that since black people are by nature good and divine, they must be separated from whites so they can avoid the latter's hour of total destruction.[69]

Over the next fifteen years, the Nation of Islam grew slowly. Then, in 1952, a young ex-convict who called himself Malcolm X came to the attention of Elijah Muhammad. Impressed with Malcolm X's faith, Muhammad soon adopted the young man as his protegé.

Articulate and intelligent, Malcolm X proved to be an effective organizer, and soon the Nation of Islam had mosques (Muslim houses of worship) established in many cities around the United States. Malcolm X's efforts were aided by the fact that urban blacks were gradually becoming convinced that whites in the North were no more inclined to accept them as equals than their Southern counterparts were. The Nation of Islam, with its message of pride in being black and its emphasis on economic self-sufficiency, began to grow rapidly.

The Nation of Islam offered many urban blacks a way out of the despair born of poverty. Through education and the religion of Islam,

Elijah Muhammad preaches to an assembly of followers from the Nation of Islam.

blacks could pull themselves out of degradation, as Malcolm X demonstrated that he had done. Malcolm X, offering his own life as an example of what was possible, said:

> I believe that it would be impossible to find anywhere in America a black man who has lived further down in the mud of human society than I have; or a black man who has been any more ignorant than I have been; or a black man who has suffered more anguish during his life than I have. But it is only after the deepest darkness that the greatest joy can come; it is only after slavery and prison that the sweetest appreciation of freedom can come.[70]

Northern blacks saw in Malcolm an intense pride in who he was. When he shared it through his preaching, it affected not only those in the Nation of Islam but all African Americans who heard his voice.

Preaching Black Pride and Militancy

Some criticized the Nation of Islam, claiming that it preached hate. Malcolm X responded by saying it was whites who had taught blacks to hate but the hatred had been turned inward:

> Who taught you to hate the texture of your hair? Who taught you to hate the color of your skin, to such an extent that you bleach it to get like the white man? Who taught you to hate yourself, from the top of your head to the soles of your feet? Who taught you to hate your own kind? Who taught you to hate the race that you belong to, so much so that you don't want to be around each other? You know, before you come asking Mr. Muhammad, does he teach hate, you should ask yourselves who taught you to hate being what God gave you. We teach you to love the hair that God gave you.[71]

To Malcolm X, the pride that he felt in being black meant that he was unwilling to turn the other cheek to oppression, as followers of the Rev. Dr. Martin Luther King's nonviolent movement were asked to do. In an interview with psychologist and author Dr. Kenneth B. Clark, Malcolm X explained his militancy:

> The Muslims who follow the Honorable Elijah Muhammad don't advocate violence, but Mister Muhammad does teach us that any human being who is intelligent has the right to defend himself. You can't take a black man who is being bitten by dogs and accuse him of advocating violence because he tries to defend himself from the bite of the dog. . . . Any Negro who

Malcolm X (right) often spoke out against the mainstream civil rights movement and its leaders, including Martin Luther King Jr. (center).

teaches Negroes to turn the other cheek in the face of attack is disarming that Negro of his God-given right, of his moral right, of his natural right, of his intelligent right to defend himself.[72]

Malcolm X often spoke out against the mainstream civil rights movement, claiming that its more conservative leaders did not speak for the urban poor. He criticized the March on Washington in 1963 saying that it accomplished little of real value to America's blacks, that it was all just for show. After the March on Washington ended, he commented:

[T]he black masses are still without land, without jobs, and without homes. . . . [T]heir Christian churches are still being bombed, their innocent little girls murdered. So what did the March on Washington accomplish? Nothing![73]

Malcolm X also criticized the speech that King delivered in Washington, D.C., now known by his repeated phrase "I Have a Dream." Instead of a dream, Malcolm X saw a nightmare. He could not share King's vision of America, that one day whites and blacks could live together in harmony and mutual respect. The teachings of Elijah Muhammad prevented him from such optimism about the white race.

He also discounted the importance of integration, doubting it would bring lasting change to the lives of African Americans. In a speech on April 8, 1964, he said:

We have to keep in mind at all times that we are not fighting for integration, nor are we fighting for separation. We are fighting for recognition as human beings. We are fighting for the right to live as free humans in this society. In fact, we are actually fighting for rights that are even greater than civil rights and that is human rights.[74]

A Change of Heart

The growth of the Nation of Islam was dealt a blow when a rift opened between Elijah Muhammad and Malcolm X as stories of Muhammad's sexual immorality began circulating. That rift widened further when Malcolm X, asked by reporters to comment on the assassination of President John F. Kennedy, said that it was an example of "chickens coming home to roost."[75] He meant that the racist, violent society that whites had created in the United States had finally claimed a notable victim, but his comment was seen by the press and most of the public as harsh and disrespectful. In response, Elijah Muhammad forbade Malcolm X to speak to the press or to preach in any mosque of the Nation of Islam for ninety days.

In March 1964, Malcolm X left the Nation of Islam and formed his own Islamic community, called the Muslim Mosque, Inc. Freed from the religious restrictions placed upon him by Elijah Muhammad, he took back much of his earlier criticism of more moderate civil rights leaders, saying:

We must find a common approach, a common solution, to a common problem. As of this minute, I've forgotten everything bad that the other leaders have said about me, and I pray they can also forget the many bad things I've said about them.[76]

In March 1964, Malcolm X left the Nation of Islam to form his own Islamic community, Muslim Mosque, Inc.

The Ballot or the Bullet

On April 3, 1964, Malcolm X delivered a speech in Cleveland, Ohio, that reflected these changes in his thinking. "The Ballot or the Bullet," as the speech has come to be known, contained elements of his militant beliefs—the bullet—while introducing his newly found spirit of cooperation with others in the civil rights movement—the ballot. This speech represents Malcolm's attempt to form an all-encompassing political vision for the civil rights movement.

Speaking only a few weeks after his official separation from the Nation of Islam and Elijah Muhammad, Malcolm X began his message to the predominantly black audience with an explanation of his religious status. He proclaimed that he was still a Muslim but did not discuss his faith or attempt to convert his listeners, fearing that such a move would divide them.

After he left the Nation of Islam, Malcolm X's message became more conciliatory.

Malcolm X hoped that his message would unify blacks and allow him to join and perhaps widen the scope of the civil rights movement to include black nationalist ideas. To that end, he compared himself to the Rev. Dr. Martin Luther King Jr., saying that although King was a Christian minister and he was a Muslim minister, their goals were essentially the same. Also, they suffered from the same oppression:

> I'm not here to argue or discuss anything we differ about, because it's time for us to submerge our differences and realize that it is best for us to first see that we have the same problem, a common problem—a problem that will make you catch hell whether you're a Baptist, or a Methodist, or a Muslim, or a nationalist. Whether you're educated or illiterate, whether you live on the boulevard or in the alley, you're going to catch hell just like I am. We're all in the same boat and we all are going to catch the same hell from the same man. He just happens to be a white man. All of us have suffered here, in this country, political oppression at the hands of the white man, economic exploitation at the hands of the white man, and social degradation at the hands of the white man.
>
> Now in speaking like this, it doesn't mean that we're anti-white, but it does mean we're anti-exploitation, we're anti-degradation, we're anti-oppression. And if the white man doesn't want us to be anti-*him*, let him stop oppressing and exploiting and degrading us.[77]

A Warning to Those Who Were to Blame

According to Malcolm X, 1964 would be crucial in the struggle for equal rights. He believed that urban blacks were running out of patience and would soon turn their backs on peaceful protest as a means of achieving the goals of the civil rights movement. He feared that violence would soon erupt in American cities. He had repeatedly warned white Americans of that danger, and in his speech, he repeated the warning:

> If we don't do something real soon, I think you'll have to agree that we're going to be forced either to use the ballot or the bullet. It's one or the other in 1964. It isn't that time is running out—time has run out! Nineteen sixty-four threatens to be the most explosive year America has ever witnessed. The most explosive year.[78]

At this point, Malcolm X could not resist pointing the finger of blame at white politicians. During election years, he claimed, whites running for office courted black voters, promising all kinds of improvements.

Once elected, though, these politicians conveniently forgot their promises. In accordance with his black nationalist philosophy, he informed the members of his audience that they could not expect much help from politicians in Washington, D.C.

Sitting at America's Table

Comparing himself to a person sitting at a dinner table without food on his plate, he questioned whether any black person in the United States could call himself or herself American:

> I'm not a politician, not even a student of politics; in fact, I'm not a student of much of anything. I'm not a Democrat, I'm not a Republican, and I don't even consider myself an American. If you and I were Americans, there'd be no problem. [Descendants of European immigrants] are already Americans. Everything that came out of Europe, every blue-eyed thing, is already American. And as long as you and I have been over here, we aren't Americans yet.
>
> Well, I am one who doesn't believe in deluding myself. I'm not going to sit at your table and watch you eat, with nothing on my plate, and call myself a diner. Sitting at the table doesn't make you a diner, unless you eat some of what's on that plate. Being here in America doesn't make you an American. Being born here in America doesn't make you an American. Why, if birth made you an American, you wouldn't need any legislation, you wouldn't need any amendments to the Constitution.[79]

Malcolm X then blasted President Lyndon B. Johnson's administration, along with Democrats and Republicans in Congress, for inaction and insincerity in addressing racial issues. He went so far as to say that many congressmen from Southern states were in violation of the Constitution—in office illegally, having been elected from states where blacks were prevented from voting.

Speaking directly to mainstream civil rights leaders about the need to expand the movement, Malcolm X said:

> The entire civil-rights struggle needs a new interpretation, a broader interpretation. . . . To those of us whose philosophy is Black Nationalism, the only way you can get involved in the civil-rights struggle is to give it a new interpretation. That old interpretation excluded us. It kept us out. So, we're giving a new interpretation . . . that will enable us to come into it, take part in it. And these handkerchief-heads who have been dillydallying

and pussyfooting and compromising—we don't intend to let them pussyfoot and dillydally and compromise any longer."⁸⁰

Advocating Violence?

Again using the analogy of ballots versus bullets, Malcolm X recounted that in Jacksonville, Florida, young blacks had used Molotov cocktails against police. That act, he said, was something new—it signaled a change in favor of violent confrontation. Paraphrasing Patrick Henry's famous Revolutionary War demand, he said, "It'll be liberty, or it will be death."⁸¹

Malcolm X advocated the use of force by blacks to defend themselves if it was necessary.

Ending his speech on a controversial note, Malcolm reiterated a statement that he had made earlier about blacks arming themselves against white oppression. To clarify his position, he said:

> The only thing that I've ever said is that in areas where the government has proven itself either unwilling or unable to defend the lives and the property of Negroes, it's time for Negroes to defend themselves. . . . It is constitutionally legal to own a rifle or a shotgun. This doesn't mean you're going to get a rifle and form battalions and go out looking for white folks, although you'd be within your rights—I mean you'd be justified; but that would be illegal and we don't do anything illegal. If the white man doesn't want the black man buying rifles and shotguns, then let the government do its job. That's all.⁸²

Discovering True Islam

The sentiments conveyed in "The Ballot or the Bullet" were not the final word on civil rights and race relations for Malcolm X. A pilgrimage to Mecca, the holiest city in Islam, made just days after the speech, transformed his attitude toward whites. Elijah Muhammad had taught his followers that white men were devils, that it was impossible for them to worship Allah. In Mecca, however, Malcolm X encountered people of all races worshiping together. Finding that true Islam welcomed all people, Malcolm X was forced to reexamine his own attitudes toward whites if he was to take the teachings of his faith seriously.

Returning to the United States, his speeches reflected this change in attitude. In a speech in Rochester, New York, on February 16, 1965, he spoke of racial unity:

> We [Muslims] don't judge a man because of the color of his skin. We don't judge you because you're white; we don't judge you because you're black; we don't judge you because you're brown. We judge you because of what you do and what you practice. . . . So we're not against white people because they're white. But we're against those who practice racism.[83]

Death and Remembrance

In New York City five days later, on Sunday, February 21, 1965, Malcolm X was to address members of a group that he had founded the previous June, the Organization of Afro-American Unity (OAAU). The purpose of the OAAU was to educate and empower black people by teaching self-defense and pride in African culture.

When Malcolm X greeted his audience with the traditional Muslim greeting "As-salaamu alaikum" ("Peace be unto you"), a struggle broke

Malcom X is comforted by his followers as he lies mortally wounded on a stage in Harlem's Audubon Ballroon on February 21, 1965.

out in the rear of the auditorium, and three men with guns ran down the aisle, fatally wounding him. The gunmen were imprisoned, but who was ultimately responsible for the assassination has never been determined to the satisfaction of Malcolm X's followers.

The obituaries for Malcolm X largely reflected the attitudes that he had adopted earlier, when he was preaching for the Nation of Islam. Writers used such phrases as "messiah of hate," a "racial agitator," "the spokesman of bitter racism," and "an extraordinary and twisted man" who had "reaped the harvest of his own philosophy" in characterizing him.[84]

The black nationalist movement did not die with Malcolm X, and the Islamic faith is well established among African Americans. The place of Malcolm X in the history of the civil rights movement and his influence on the psychological makeup of today's African Americans are still being debated, however. According to James H. Cone, the consciousness of black America was transformed by the unswerving pride that Malcolm X had in himself and in his race:

> Blacks today who are proud to claim their African heritage should thank Malcolm. More than anyone else he created the space for them to affirm their blackness. More than anyone else he taught blacks that there can be no freedom for the members of the African American community in the United States without self-esteem, a high regard for themselves as a *black* people.[85]

Or, as another person who knew him, James 67X Shabazz, put it, "Malcolm's thoughts will only die when all people—especially of African origin—are free as Malcolm wanted us to be."[86]

Appendix

Document 1: Booker T. Washington's "Cast Down Your Bucket"

Booker T. Washington delivered his "Cast Down Your Bucket" speech on September 18, 1895, at the opening of the Cotton States and International Exposition in Atlanta, Georgia. Washington, founder of the Tuskegee Institute, was asked to address the mostly white crowd about the accomplishments of his race and the future of the Negro in the United States. In his speech, he urged compromise, rather than confrontation, to achieve equality for African Americans.

Mr. President and Gentlemen of the Board of Directors and Citizens: One-third of the population of the South is of the Negro race. No enterprise seeking the material, civil, or moral welfare of this section can disregard this element of our population and reach the highest success. I but convey to you, Mr. President and Directors, the sentiment of the masses of my race when I say that in no way have the value and manhood of the American Negro been more fittingly and generously recognized than by the managers of this magnificent Exposition at every stage of its progress. It is a recognition that will do more to cement the friendship of the two races than any occurrence since the dawn of freedom.

Not only this, but the opportunity here afforded will awaken among us a new era of industrial progress. Ignorant and inexperienced it is not strange that in the first years of our new life we began at the top instead of at the bottom; that a seat in Congress or the State Legislature was more sought than real estate or industrial skill; that the political convention or stump speaking had more attractions than starting a dairy farm or truck garden.

A ship lost at sea for many days suddenly sighted a friendly vessel. From the mast of the unfortunate vessel was seen a signal, "Water, water; we die of thirst!" The answer from the friendly vessel at once came back: "Cast down your bucket where you are." A second time the signal, "Water, water; send us water!" ran up from the distressed vessel, and was answered: "Cast down your bucket where you are." The captain of the distressed vessel, at last heeding the injunction, cast down his bucket, and it came up full of fresh, sparkling water from the mouth of the Amazon River. To those of my race who depend upon bettering their condition in a foreign land, or who underestimate the importance of cultivating friendly relations with the Southern white man, who is his next door neighbor, I would say: "Cast down your bucket where you are"—cast it down in making friends in every manly way of the people of all races by whom we are surrounded.

Cast it down in agriculture, mechanics, in commerce, in domestic service, and in the professions. And in this connection it is well to bear in mind that whatever other sins the South may be called to bear, when it comes to business, pure and simple, it is in the South that the Negro is given a man's chance in the commercial world, and in nothing is this Exposition more eloquent than in emphasizing this chance. Our greatest danger is, that in the great leap from slavery to freedom we may overlook the fact that the masses of us are to live by the productions of our hands, and fail to keep in mind that we shall prosper in proportion as we learn to dignify and glorify common labor, and put brains and skill into the common occupations of life; shall prosper in proportion as we learn to draw the line between the superficial and the substantial, the ornamental gewgaws of life and the useful. No race can prosper till it learns that there is as much dignity in tilling a field as in writing a poem. It is at the bottom of life we must begin, and not at the top. Nor should we permit our grievances to overshadow our opportunities.

To those of the white race who look to the incoming of those of foreign birth and strange tongue and habits for the prosperity of the South, were I permitted I would repeat what I say to my own race, "Cast down your bucket where you are." Cast it down among the 8,000,000 Negroes whose habits you know, whose fidelity and love you have tested in days when to have proved treacherous meant the ruin of your firesides. Cast down your bucket among these people who have, without strikes and labor wars, tilled your fields, cleared your forests, builded your railroads and cities, and brought forth treasures from the bowels of the earth, and helped make possible this magnificent representation of the progress of the South. Casting down your bucket among my people, helping and encouraging them as you are doing on these grounds, and, with education of head, hand and heart, you will find that they will buy your surplus land, make blossom the waste places in your fields, and run your factories. While doing this, you can be sure in the future, as in the past, that you and your families will be surrounded by the most patient, faithful, law-abiding, and unresentful people that the world has seen. As we have proved our loyalty to you in the past, in nursing your children, watching by the sick bed of your mothers and fathers, and often following them with tear-dimmed eyes to their graves, so in the future, in our humble way, we shall stand by you with a devotion that no foreigner can approach, ready to lay down our lives, if need be, in defense of yours, interlacing our industrial, commercial, civil, and religious life with yours in a way that shall make the interests of both races one. In all things that are purely social we can be as separate as the fingers, yet one as the hand in all things essential to mutual progress.

There is no defense or security for any of us except in the highest intelligence and development of all. If anywhere there are efforts tending to curtail the fullest growth of the Negro, let these efforts be turned into stimulating, encouraging, and making him the most useful and intelligent citizen. Effort or means so invested will pay a thousand per cent interest. These efforts will be twice blessed—blessing him that gives and him that takes.

There is no escape through law of man or God from the inevitable:

> The laws of changeless justice bind
> Oppressor with oppressed;
> And close as sin and suffering joined
> We march to fate abreast.

Nearly sixteen millions of hands will aid you in pulling the load upwards or they will pull against you the load downwards. We shall constitute one-third and more of the ignorance and crime of the South, or one-third its intelligence and progress; we shall contribute one-third to the business and industrial prosperity of the South, or we shall prove a veritable body of death, stagnating, depressing, retarding every effort to advance the body politic.

Gentlemen of the Exposition, as we present to you our humble effort at an exhibition of our progress, you must not expect overmuch. Starting thirty years ago with ownership here and there in a few quilts and pumpkins and chickens (gathered from miscellaneous sources), remember the path that has led from these to the invention and production of agricultural implements, buggies, steam engines, newspapers, books, statuary, carving, paintings, the management of drug stores and banks has not been trodden without contact with thorns and thistles. While we take pride in what we exhibit as a result of our independent efforts, we do not for a moment forget that our part in this exhibition would fall far short of your expectations but for the constant help that has come to our educational life, not only from the Southern States, but especially from Northern philanthropists, who have made their gifts a constant stream of blessing and encouragement.

The wisest among my race understand that the agitation of questions of social equality is the extremest folly. and that progress in the enjoyment of all the privileges that will come to us must be the result of severe and constant struggle rather than of artificial forcing. No race that has anything to contribute to the markets of the world is long in any degree ostracized. It is important and right that all privileges of the law be ours, but it is vastly more important that we be prepared for the exercise of those privileges. The opportunity to earn a dollar in a factory just now is worth infinitely more than the opportunity to spend a dollar in an opera house.

In conclusion, may I repeat that nothing in thirty years has given us more hope and encouragement, and drawn us so near to you of the white race, as this opportunity offered by the Exposition; and here bending, as it were, over the altar that represents the results of the struggles of your race and mine, both starting practically empty-handed three decades ago, I pledge that, in your effort to work out the great and intricate problem which God has laid at the doors of the South, you shall have at all times the patient, sympathetic help of my race; only let this be constantly in mind that, while from representations in these buildings of the products of field, of forest, of mine, of factory, letters, and art, much good will come, yet far above and beyond material benefits will be the higher good, that let us pray God will come, in a blotting out of sectional differences and racial animosities and suspicions, in a determination to administer absolute justice, in a willing obedience among all classes to the mandates of law. This, coupled with our material prosperity, will bring into our beloved South a new heaven and a new earth.

Document 2: Thurgood Marshall's closing arguments in *Brown v. Board of Education*

One of the most far-reaching Supreme Court decisions of the twentieth century was Brown vs. the Board of Education of Topeka, Kansas. *Leading up to this monumental decision were decades of legal battles fought on behalf of African Americans by the NAACP Legal Defense Fund (LDF). On December 7, 1953, these efforts reached a climax when Thurgood Marshall, Director of the LDF, and later a Supreme Court justice, addressed the Court. His powerful closing argument, urging desegregation of public schools in the United States, helped sway the nine justices.*

It follows that with education, this Court has made segregation and inequality equivalent concepts. They have equal rating, equal footing, and if segregation thus necessarily imports inequality, it makes no great difference whether we say that the Negro is wronged because he received unequal treatment. . . .

And finally I would like to say that each lawyer on the other side has made it clear as to what the position of the state was on this, and it would be all right possibly but for the fact that this is so crucial. There is no way you can repay lost school years.

These children in these cases are guaranteed by the states some twelve years of education in varying degrees, and this idea, if I understand it, to leave it to the states until they work it out—and I think that is the most ingenious argument—you leave it to the states, they say, and then they say that the states haven't done anything about it in a hundred years, so for that reason this Court doesn't touch it.

The argument of judicial restraint has no application in this case. There is a relationship between federal and state, but there is no corollary or relationship as to the Fourteenth Amendment.

The duty of enforcing, the duty of following the Fourteenth Amendment, is placed upon the states. The duty of enforcing the Fourteenth Amendment is placed upon this Court, and the argument that they make over and over again to my mind is the same type of argument they charge us with making, the same argument Charles Sumner made. Possibly so.

And we hereby charge them with making the same argument that was made before the Civil War, the same argument that was made during the period between the ratification of the Fourteenth Amendment and the *Plessy v. Ferguson* case.

And I think it makes no progress for us to find out who made what argument. It is our position that whether or not you base this case solely on the intent of Congress or whether you base it on the logical extension of the doctrine as set forth in the McLaurin case, on either basis the same conclusion is required, which is that this Court makes it clear to all of these states that in administering their governmental functions, at least those that are vital not to the life of the state alone, not to the country alone, but vital to the world in general, that little pet feelings of race, little pet feelings of custom—I got the feeling on hearing the discussion yesterday that when you put a white child in a school with a whole lot of colored children, the child would fall apart or something. Everybody knows that is not true.

Those same kids in Virginia and South Carolina—and I have seen them do it—they play in the streets together, they play on their farms together, they go down the road together, they separate to go to school, they come out of school and play ball together. They have to be separated in school.

There is some magic to it. You can have them voting together, you can have them not restricted because of law in the houses they live in. You can have them going to the same state university and the same college, but if they go to elementary and high school, the world will fall apart. And it is the exact same argument that has been made to this Court over and over again, and we submit that when they charge us with making the legislative argument, it is in truth they who are making the legislative argument.

They can't take race out of this case. From the day this case was filed until this moment, nobody has in any form or fashion, despite the fact I made it clear in the opening argument that I was relying on it, done anything to distinguish this statute from the Black Codes, which they must admit, because nobody can dispute, say anything anybody wants to say, one way or the other, the Fourteenth Amendment was intended to deprive the states of power to enforce Black Codes or anything else like it.

We charge that they are Black Codes. They obviously are Black Codes if you read them. They haven't denied that they are Black Codes, so if the Court wants to very narrowly decided this case, they can decide it on that point.

So whichever way it is done, the only way that this Court can decide this case in opposition to our position, is that there must be some reason which gives the state the right to make a classification that they can make in regard to nothing else in regard to Negroes, and we submit the only way to arrive at that decision is to find that for some reason Negroes are inferior to all other human beings.

Nobody will stand in the Court and urge that, and in order to arrive at the decision that they want us to arrive at, there would have to be some recognition of a reason why of all of the multitudinous groups of people in this country you have to single out Negroes and give them this separate treatment.

It can't be because of slavery in the past, because there are very few groups in this country that haven't had slavery some place back in history of their groups. It can't be color because there are Negroes as white as the drifted snow, with blue eyes, and they are just as segregated as the colored man.

The only thing can be is an inherent determination that the people who were formerly in slavery, regardless of anything else, shall be kept as near that stage as is possible, and now is the time, we submit, that this Court should make it clear that that is not what our Constitution stands for.

Thank you, sir.

Document 3: Dr. Martin Luther King's "Letter from Birmingham Jail"

None of Dr. Martin Luther King's statements during the American civil rights movement, either written or spoken, explain in more detail, or with more eloquence, the plight of African Americans, and the need for nonviolent protest, than his "Letter from Birmingham Jail," dated April 6, 1963. King, in jail for his participation in protests in the city, wrote the letter from his cell in answer to an editorial written by white clergymen in Birmingham, Alabama, questioning the movement's methods.

While confined here in the Birmingham city jail, I came across your recent statement calling my present activities "unwise and untimely." Seldom do I pause to answer criticism of my work and ideas. If I sought to answer all the criticisms that cross my desk, my secretaries would have little time for anything other than such correspondence in the course of the day, and I would have no time for constructive work. But since I feel that you are men of genuine good will and that your criticisms are sincerely set forth, I want to try to answer your statements in what I hope will be patient and reasonable terms.

I think I should indicate why I am here in Birmingham, since you have been influenced by the view which argues against "outsiders coming in." I have the honor of serving as president of the Southern Christian Leadership Conference, an organization operating in every southern state, with headquarters in Atlanta, Georgia. We have some eighty-five affiliated organizations across the South, and one of them is the Alabama Christian Movement for Human Rights. Frequently we share staff, educational and financial resources with our affiliates. Several months ago the affiliate here in Birmingham asked us to be on call to engage in a nonviolent direct-action program if such were deemed necessary. We readily consented, and when the hour came we lived up to our promise. So I, along with several members of my staff, am here because I was invited here. I am here because I have organizational ties here.

But more basically, I am in Birmingham because injustice is here. Just as the prophets of the eighth century B.C. left their villages and carried their "thus saith the Lord" far beyond the boundaries of their home towns, and just as the Apostle Paul left his village of Tarsus and carried the gospel of Jesus Christ to the far corners of the Greco-Roman world, so am I compelled to carry the gospel of freedom beyond my own home town. Like Paul, I must constantly respond to the Macedonian call for aid.

Moreover, I am cognizant of the interrelatedness of all communities and states. I cannot sit idly by in Atlanta and not be concerned about what happens in Birmingham. Injustice anywhere is a threat to justice everywhere. We are caught in an inescapable network of mutuality, tied in a single garment of destiny. Whatever affects one directly, affects all indirectly. Never again can we afford to live with the narrow, provincial "outside agitator" idea. Anyone who lives inside the United States can never be considered an outsider anywhere within its bounds.

You deplore the demonstrations taking place in Birmingham. But your statement, I am sorry to say, fails to express a similar concern for the conditions that brought about the demonstrations. I am sure that none of you would want to rest content with the superficial kind of social analysis that deals merely with effects and does not grapple with underlying causes. It is unfortunate that demonstrations are taking place in Birmingham, but it is even more unfortunate that the city's white power structure left the Negro community with no alternative.

In any nonviolent campaign there are four basic steps: collection of the facts to determine whether injustices exist; negotiation; self-purification; and direct action. We have gone through all these steps in Birmingham. There can be no gainsaying the fact that racial injustice engulfs this community. Birmingham is probably the most thoroughly segregated city in the United States. Its ugly record of brutality is widely known. Negroes have experienced grossly unjust treatment in the courts. There have been more unsolved bombings of Negro homes and churches in Birmingham than in any other city in the nation. These are the hard, brutal facts of the case. On the basis of these conditions, Negro leaders sought to negotiate with the city fathers. But the latter consistently refused to engage in good-faith negotiation. . . .

[Omitted here are three paragraphs describing unsuccessful negotiations with merchants to remove racial signs from stores, and strategies for timing the direct action campaign which followed.]

You may well ask: "Why direct action? Why sit-ins, marches and so forth? Isn't negotiation a better path?" You are quite right in calling for negotiation. Indeed, this is the very purpose of direct action. Nonviolent direct action seeks to create such a crisis and foster such a tension that a community which has constantly refused to negotiate is forced to confront the issue. It seeks so to dramatize the issue that it can no longer be ignored. My citing the creation of tension as part of the work of the nonviolent-resister may sound rather shocking. But I must confess that I am not afraid of the word "tension." I have earnestly opposed violent tension, but there is a type of constructive, nonviolent tension which is necessary for growth. Just as Socrates felt that it was necessary to create a tension in the mind so that individuals could rise from the bondage of myths and half-truths to the unfettered realm of creative analysis and objective appraisal, so must we see the need for nonviolent gadflies to create the kind of tension in society that will help men rise from the dark depths of prejudice and racism to the majestic heights of understanding and brotherhood.

The purpose of our direct-action program is to create a situation so crisis-packed that it will inevitably open the door to negotiation. I therefore concur with you in your call for negotiation. Too long has our beloved Southland been bogged down in a tragic effort to live in monologue rather than dialogue.

One of the basic points in your statement is that the action that I and my associates have taken in Birmingham is untimely. . . . My friends, I must say to you that we have not made a single gain in civil rights without determined legal and nonviolent pressure. Lamentably, it is an historical fact that privileged groups seldom give up their privileges voluntarily. Individuals may see the moral light and voluntarily give up their unjust posture; but, as Reinhold Niebuhr has reminded us, groups tend to be more immoral than individuals.

We know through painful experience that freedom is never voluntarily given by the oppressor; it must be demanded by the oppressed. Frankly, I have yet to engage in a direct-action campaign that was "well timed" in the view of those who have not suffered unduly from the disease of segregation. For years now I have heard the word "Wait!" It rings in the ear of every Negro with piercing familiarity. This "Wait" has almost always meant "Never." We must come to see, with one of our distinguished jurists, that "justice too long delayed is justice denied."

We have waited for more than 340 years for our constitutional and God-given rights. The nations of Asia and Africa are moving with jetlike speed toward gaining political independence, but we still creep at horse-and-buggy pace toward gaining a cup of coffee at a lunch counter. Perhaps it is easy for those who have never felt the stinging darts of segregation to say, "Wait." But when you have seen vicious mobs lynch your mothers and fathers at will and drown your sisters and brothers at whim; when you have seen hate-filled policemen curse, kick and even kill your black brothers and sisters; when you see the vast majority of your twenty million Negro brothers smothering in an airtight cage of poverty in the midst of an affluent society; when you suddenly find your tongue twisted and your speech stammering as you seek to explain to your six-year-old daughter why she can't go to the public amusement park that has just been advertised on television, and see tears welling up in her eyes when she is told that Funtown is closed to colored children, and see ominous clouds of inferiority beginning to form in her little mental sky, and see her beginning to distort her personality by developing an unconscious bitterness toward white people; when you have to concoct an answer for a five-year-old son who is asking: "Daddy, why do white people treat colored people so mean?"; when you take a cross-country drive and find it necessary to sleep night after night in the uncomfortable corners of your automobile because no motel will accept you; when you are humiliated day in and day out by nagging signs reading "white" and "colored"; when your first name becomes "nigger," your middle name becomes "boy" (however old you are) and your last name becomes "John," and your wife and mother are never given the respected title "Mrs."; when you are harried by day and haunted by night by the fact that you are a Negro, living constantly at tiptoe stance, never quite knowing what to expect next, and are plagued with inner fears and outer resentments; when you are forever fighting a degenerating sense of "nobodiness"—then you will understand why we find it difficult to wait. There comes a time when the cup of endurance runs over, and men are no longer willing to be plunged into the abyss of despair. I hope, sirs, you can understand our legitimate and unavoidable impatience.

You express a great deal of anxiety over our willingness to break laws. This is certainly a legitimate concern. Since we so diligently urge people to obey the Supreme Court's decision of 1954 outlawing segregation in the public schools, at first glance it may seem rather paradoxical for us consciously to break laws. One may well ask: "How can you advocate breaking some laws and obeying others?" The answer lies in the fact that there are two types of laws: just and unjust. I would be the first to advocate obeying just laws. One has not only a legal but a moral responsibility to obey just laws. Conversely, one has a moral responsibility to disobey unjust laws. I would agree with St. Augustine that "an unjust law is no law at all."

Now, what is the difference between the two? How does one determine whether a law is just or unjust? A just law is a man-made code that squares with the moral law or the law of God. An unjust law is a code that is out of harmony with the moral law. To put it in the terms of St. Thomas Aquinas: An unjust law is a human law that is not rooted in eternal law and natural law. Any law that uplifts human personality is just. Any law that degrades human personality is unjust. All segregation statutes are unjust because segregation distorts the soul and damages the personality. It gives the segregator a false sense of superiority and the segregated a false sense of inferiority. Segregation, to use the terminology of the Jewish philosopher Martin Buber, substitutes an "I-it" relationship for an "I-thou" relationship and ends up relegating persons to the status of things. Hence segregation is not only politically, economically and sociologically unsound, it is morally wrong and awful. Paul Tillich said that sin is separation. Is not segregation an existential expression of man's tragic separation, his awful estrangement, his terrible sinfulness? Thus it is that I can urge men to obey the 1954 decision of the Supreme Court, for it is morally right; and I can urge them to disobey segregation ordinances, for they are morally wrong.

Let us consider a more concrete example of just and unjust laws. An unjust law is a code that a numerical or power majority group compels a minority group to obey but does not make binding on itself. This is *difference* made legal. By the same token, a just law is a code that a majority compels a minority to follow and that it is willing to follow itself. This is sameness made legal.

Let me give another explanation. A law is unjust if it is inflicted on a minority that, as a result of being denied the right to vote, had no part in enacting or devising the law. Who can say that the legislature of Alabama which set up that state's segregation laws was democratically elected? Throughout Alabama all sorts of devious methods are used to prevent Negroes from becoming registered voters, and there are some counties in which, even though Negroes constitute a majority of the population, not a single Negro is registered. Can any law enacted under such circumstances be considered democratically structured?

Sometimes a law is just on its face and unjust in its application. For instance, I have been arrested on a charge of parading without a permit. Now, there is nothing wrong in having an ordinance which requires a permit for a parade. But such an ordinance becomes unjust when it is used to maintain segregation and to deny citizens the First Amendment privilege of peaceful assembly and protest.

I hope you are able to see the distinction I am trying to point out. In no sense do I advocate evading or defying the law, as would the rabid segregationist. That would lead to anarchy. One who breaks an unjust law must do so openly, lovingly, and with a willingness to accept the penalty. I submit that an individual who breaks a law that conscience tells him is unjust and who willingly accepts the penalty of imprisonment in order to arouse the conscience of the community over its injustice, is in reality expressing the highest respect for law.

Of course, there is nothing new about this kind of civil disobedience. It was evidenced sublimely in the refusal of Shadrach, Meshach and Abednego to obey the laws of Nebuchadnezzar, on the ground that a higher moral law was at stake. It was practiced superbly by the early Christians, who were willing to face hungry lions and the excruciating pain of chopping blocks rather than submit to certain unjust laws of the Roman Empire. To a degree, academic freedom is a reality today because Socrates practiced civil disobedience. In our own nation, the Boston Tea Party represented a massive act of civil disobedience.

We should never forget that everything Adolf Hitler did in Germany was "legal" and everything the Hungarian freedom fighters did in Hungary was "illegal." It was "illegal" to aid and comfort a Jew in Hitler's Germany. Even so, I am sure that, had I lived in Germany at the time, I would have aided and comforted my Jewish brothers. If today I lived in a Communist country where certain principles dear to the Christian faith are suppressed, I would openly advocate disobeying that country's antireligious laws.

I must make two honest confessions to you, my Christian and Jewish brothers. First, I must confess that over the past few years I have been gravely disappointed with the white moderate. I have almost reached the regrettable conclusion that the Negro's great stumbling block in his stride toward freedom is not the White Citizen's Counciler or the Ku Klux Klanner, but the white moderate, who is more devoted to "order" than to justice; who prefers a negative peace which is the absence of tension to a positive peace which is the presence of justice; who constantly says: "I agree with you in the goal you seek, but I cannot agree with your methods of direct action"; who paternalistically believes he can set the timetable for another man's freedom; who lives by a mythical concept of time and who constantly advises the Negro to wait for a "more convenient season." Shallow understanding from people of good will is more frustrating than absolute misunderstanding from people of ill will. Lukewarm acceptance is much more bewildering than outright rejection.

I had hoped that the white moderate would understand that law and order exist for the purpose of establishing justice and that when they fail in this purpose they become the dangerously structured dams that block the flow of social progress. I had hoped that the white moderate would understand that the present tension in the South is a necessary phase of the transition from an obnoxious negative peace, in which the Negro passively accepted his unjust plight, to a substantive and positive peace, in which all men will respect the dignity and worth of human personality. Actually, we who engage in nonviolent direct action are not the creators of tension. We merely bring to the surface the hidden tension that is already alive. We bring it out in the open, where it can be seen and dealt with. Like a boil that can never be cured so long as it is covered up but must be opened with all its ugliness to the natural medicines of air and light, injustice must be exposed, with all the tension its exposure creates, to the light of human conscience and the air of national opinion before it can be cured.

In your statement you assert that our actions, even though peaceful, must be condemned because they precipitate violence. But is this a logical assertion? Isn't this like condemning a robbed man because his possession of money precipitated the evil act of robbery? Isn't this like condemning Socrates because his unswerving commitment to truth and his philosophical inquiries precipitated the act by the misguided populace in which they made him drink hemlock? Isn't this like condemning Jesus because his unique God-consciousness and never-ceasing devotion to God's will precipitated the evil act of crucifixion? We must come to see that, as the federal courts have consistently affirmed, it is wrong to urge an individual to cease his efforts to gain his basic constitutional rights because the quest may precipitate violence. Society must protect the robbed and punish the robber. . . .

[Omitted here is one paragraph expressing disappointed hope "that the white moderate would reject the myth of time"—i.e., the idea that man's lot inevitably improves, irrespective of actions performed for good or evil.]

You speak of our activity in Birmingham as extreme. At first I was rather disappointed that fellow clergymen would see my nonviolent efforts as those of an extremist. I began thinking about the fact that I stand in the middle of two opposing forces in the Negro community. One is a force of complacency, made up in part of Negroes who, as a result of long years of oppression, are so drained of self-respect and a sense of "somebodiness" that they have adjusted to segregation; and in part of a few middle class Negroes who, because of a degree of academic and economic security and because in some ways they profit by segregation, have become insensitive to the problems of the masses. The other force is one of bitterness and hatred, and it comes perilously close to advocating violence. It is expressed in the various black nationalist groups that are springing up across the nation, the largest and best-known being Elijah Muhammad's Muslim movement. Nourished by the Negro's frustration over the continued existence of racial discrimination, this movement is made up of people who have lost faith in America, who have absolutely repudiated Christianity, and who have concluded that the white man is an incorrigible "devil."

I have tried to stand between these two forces, saying that we need emulate neither the "do-nothingism" of the complacent nor the hatred and despair of the black nationalist. For there is the more excellent way of love and nonviolent protest. I am grateful to God that, through the influence of the Negro church, the way of nonviolence became an integral part of our struggle.

If this philosophy had not emerged, by now many streets of the South would, I am convinced, be flowing with blood. And I am further convinced that if our white brothers dismiss as "rabble-rousers" and "outside agitators" those of us who employ nonviolent direct action, and if they refuse to support our nonviolent efforts, millions of Negroes will, out of frustration and despair, seek solace and security in black-nationalist ideologies—a development that would inevitably lead to a frightening racial nightmare.

Oppressed people cannot remain oppressed forever. The yearning for freedom eventually manifests itself, and that is what has happened to the American Negro. Something within has reminded him of his birthright of freedom, and something without has reminded him that it can be gained. Consciously or unconsciously, he has been caught up by the *Zeitgeist*, and with his black brothers of Africa and his brown and yellow brothers of Asia, South America and the Caribbean, the United States Negro is moving with a sense of great urgency toward the promised land of racial justice. If one recognizes this vital urge that has engulfed the Negro community, one should readily understand why public demonstrations are taking place. The Negro has many pent-up resentments and latent frustrations, and he must release them. So let him march; let him make prayer pilgrimages to the city hall; let him go on freedom rides—and try to understand why he must do so. If his repressed emotions are not released in nonviolent ways, they will seek expression through violence; this is not a threat but a fact of history. So I have not said to my people: "Get rid of your discontent." Rather, I have tried to say that this normal and healthy discontent can be channeled into the creative outlet of nonviolent direct action. And now this approach is being termed extremist.

But though I was initially disappointed at being categorized as an extremist, as I continued to think about the matter I gradually gained a measure of satisfaction from the label. Was not Jesus an extremist for love: "Love your enemies, bless them that curse you, do good to them that hate you, and pray for them which despitefully use you, and persecute you." Was not Amos an extremist for justice: "Let justice roll down like waters and righteousness like an ever-flowing stream." Was not Paul an extremist for the Christian gospel: "I bear in my body the marks of the Lord Jesus." Was not Martin Luther an extremist: "Here I stand; I cannot do otherwise, so help me God." And John Bunyan: "I will stay in jail to the end of my days before I make a butchery of my conscience." And Abraham Lincoln: "This nation cannot survive half slave and half free." And Thomas Jefferson: "We hold these truths to be self-evident, that all men are created equal . . ." So the question is not whether we will be extremists, but what kind of extremists we will be. Will we be extremists for hate or for love? Will we be extremists for the preservation of injustice or for the extension of justice? In that dramatic scene on Calvary's hill three men were crucified. We must never forget that all three were crucified for the same crime—the crime of extremism. Two were extremists for immorality, and thus fell below their environment. The other, Jesus Christ, was an extremist for love, truth and goodness, and thereby rose above his environment. Perhaps the South, the nation and the world are in dire need of creative extremists.

I had hoped that the white moderate would see this need. Perhaps I was too optimistic; perhaps I expected too much. I suppose I should have realized that few members of the oppressor race can understand the deep groans and passionate yearnings of the oppressed race, and still fewer have the vision to see that injustice must be rooted out by strong, persistent and determined action. I am thankful, however, that some of our white brothers in the South have grasped the meaning of this social revolution and committed themselves to it. They are still too few in quantity, but they are big in quality. Some—such as Ralph McGill, Lillian Smith, Harry Golden, James McBride Dabbs, Ann Braden and Sarah Patton Boyle—have written about our struggle in eloquent and prophetic terms. Others have marched with us down nameless streets of the South. They have languished in filthy, roach-infested jails, suffering the abuse and brutality of policemen who view them as "dirty nigger lovers." Unlike so many of their moderate brothers and sisters, they have recognized the urgency of the moment and sensed the need for powerful "action" antidotes to combat the disease of segregation. . . .

[Omitted here is King's second confession: eleven paragraphs expressing his dissatisfaction "with the white Church and its leadership."]

But even if the church does not come to the aid of justice, I have no despair about the future. I have no fear about the outcome of our struggle in Birmingham, even if our motives are at present misunderstood. We will reach the goal of freedom in Birmingham, and all over the nation, because the goal of America is freedom. Abused and scorned though we may be, our destiny is tied up with America's destiny. Before the pilgrims landed at Plymouth, we were here. Before the pen of Jefferson etched the majestic words of the Declaration of Independence across the pages of history, we were here. For more than two centuries our forebears labored in this country without wages; they made cotton king; they built the homes of their masters while suffering gross injustice and shameful humiliation—and yet out of a bottomless vitality they continued to thrive and develop. If the inexpressible cruelties of slavery could not stop us, the opposition we now face will surely fail. We will win our freedom because the sacred heritage of our nation and the eternal will of God are embodied in our echoing demands.

Before closing I feel impelled to mention one other point in your statement that has troubled me profoundly. You warmly commended the Birmingham police force for keeping "order" and "preventing violence." I doubt that you would have so warmly commended the police force if you had seen its dogs sinking their teeth into unarmed, nonviolent Negroes. I doubt that you would so quickly commend the policemen if you were to observe their ugly and inhumane treatment of Negroes here in the city jail; if you were to watch them push and curse old Negro women and young Negro girls; if you were to see them slap and kick old Negro men and young boys; if you were to observe them, as they did on two occasions, refuse to give us food because we wanted to sing our grace together. I cannot join you in your praise of the Birmingham police department.

It is true that the police have exercised a degree of discipline in handling the demonstrators. In this sense they have conducted themselves rather "nonviolently" in public. But for what purpose? To preserve the evil system of segregation. Over the past few years I have consistently preached that nonviolence demands that the means we use must be as pure as the ends we seek. I have tried to make clear that it is wrong to use immoral means to attain moral ends. . . . As T. S. Eliot has said: "The last temptation is the greatest treason: To do the right deed for the wrong reason."

I wish you had commended the Negro sit-inners and demonstrators of Birmingham for their sublime courage, their willingness to suffer and their amazing discipline in the midst of great provocation. One day the South will recognize its real heroes. They will be the James Merediths, with the noble sense of purpose that enables them to face jeering, and hostile mobs, and with the agonizing loneliness that characterizes the life of the pioneer. They will be old, oppressed, battered Negro women, symbolized in a seventy-two-year-old woman in Montgomery, Alabama, who rose up with a sense of dignity and with her people decided not to ride segregated buses, and who responded with ungrammatical profundity to one who inquired about her weariness: "My feets is tired, but my soul is at rest." They will be the young high school and college students, the young ministers of the gospel and a host of their elders, courageously and nonviolently sitting in at lunch counters and willingly going to jail for conscience' sake. One day the South will know that when these disinherited children of God sat down at lunch counters, they were in reality standing up for what is best in the American dream and for the most sacred values in our Judaeo-Christian heritage, thereby bringing our nation back to those great wells of democracy which were dug deep by the founding fathers in their formulation of the Constitution and the Declaration of Independence.

Never before have I written so long a letter. I'm afraid it is much too long to take your precious time. I can assure you that it would have been much shorter if I had been writing from a comfortable desk, but what else can one do when he is alone in a narrow jail cell, other than write long letters, think long thoughts and pray long prayers?

If I have said anything in this letter that overstates the truth and indicates an unreasonable impatience, I beg you to forgive me. If I have said anything that understates the truth and indicates my having a patience that allows me to settle for anything less than brotherhood, I beg God to forgive me.

I hope this letter finds you strong in the faith. I also hope that circumstances will soon make it possible for me to meet each of you, not as an integrationist or a civil rights leader but as a fellow clergyman and a Christian brother. Let us all hope that the dark clouds of racial prejudice will soon pass away and the deep fog of misunderstanding will be lifted from our fear-drenched communities, and in some not too distant tomorrow the radiant stars of love and brotherhood will shine over our great nation with all their scintillating beauty.

Yours for the cause of Peace and Brotherhood, Martin Luther King, Jr.

Reprinted by arrangement with the Heirs of the Estate of Martin Luther King Jr. c/o The Writers House, Inc., as agents for the proprietor.

Document 4: Fannie Lou Hamer's testimony at the Democratic National Convention in 1964

Fannie Lou Hamer, a Mississippi sharecropper and political activist, spoke simply and eloquently before the Credentials Committee at the Democratic National Convention on August 22, 1964. She and others were trying to gain convention seating for delegates of the Mississippi Freedom Democratic Party, protesting African American exclusion from the delegate selection process in Mississippi. Her nationally televised testimony, about the treatment of blacks in the South who tried to register to vote, stunned the nation.

Mr. Chairman, and the Credentials Committee, my name is Mrs. Fannie Lou Hamer, and I live at 626 East Lafayette Street, Ruleville, Mississippi, Sunflower County, the home of Senator James O. Eastland, and Senator Stennis.

It was the 31st of August in 1962 that eighteen of us traveled twenty-six miles to the county courthouse in Indianola to try to register to try to become first-class citizens. We was met in Indianola by Mississippi men, highway patrolmens, and they only allowed two of us in to take the literacy test at the time. After we had taken this test and started back to Ruleville, we was held up by the City Police and the State Highway Patrolmen and carried back to Indianola, where the bus driver was charged that day with driving a bus the wrong color.

After we paid the fine among us, we continued on to Ruleville, and Reverend Jeff Sunny carried me four miles in the rural area where I had worked as a timekeeper and sharecropper for eighteen years. I was met there by my children, who told me the plantation owner was angry because I had gone down to try to register. After they told me, my husband came, and said the plantation owner was raising cane because I had tried to register, and before he quit talking the plantation owner came, and said, "Fannie Lou, do you know—did Pap tell you what I said?"

I said, "Yes, sir."

He said, "I mean that," he said. "If you don't go down and withdraw your registration, you will have to leave," said, "Then if you go down and withdraw," he said. "You will—you might have to go because we are not ready for that in Mississippi."

And I addressed him and told him and said, "I didn't try to register for you. I tried to register for myself." I had to leave that same night.

On the 10th of September, 1962, sixteen bullets was fired into the home of Mr. and Mrs. Robert Tucker for me. That same night two girls were shot in Ruleville, Mississippi. Also Mr. Joe McDonald's house was shot in.

And in June, the 9th, 1963, I had attended a voter-registration workshop, was returning back to Mississippi. Ten of us was traveling by the Continental Trailway bus. When we got to Winona, Mississippi, which is Montgomery County, four of the people got off to use the washroom, and two of the people—to use the restaurant—two of the people wanted to use the washroom. The four people that had gone in to use the restaurant was ordered out. During this time I was on the bus. But when I looked through the window and saw they had rushed out, I got off of the bus to see what had happened, and one of the ladies said, "It was a state highway patrolman and a chief of police ordered us out."

I got back on the bus and one of the persons had used the washroom got back on the bus, too. As soon as I was seated on the bus, I saw when they began to get the four people in a highway patrolman's car. I stepped off the bus to see what was happening and somebody screamed from the car that the four workers was in and said, "Get that one there," and when I went to get in the car, when the man told me I was under arrest, he kicked me.

I was carried to the county jail, and put in the booking room. They left some of the people in the booking room and began to place us in cells. I was placed in a cell with a young woman called Miss Euvester Simpson. After I was placed in the cell I began to hear sounds of licks and screams. I could hear the sounds of licks and horrible screams, and I could hear somebody say, "Can you say, yes sir, nigger? Can you say yes, sir?"

And they would say other horrible names. She would say, "Yes, I can say yes, sir."

"So say it."

She says, "I don't know you well enough."

They beat her, I don't know how long, and after a while she began to pray, and asked God to have mercy on those people.

And it wasn't too long before three white men came to my cell. One of these men was a State Highway Patrolman and he asked me where I was from, and I told him Ruleville. He said, "We are going to check this." And they left my cell and it wasn't too long before they came back. He said, "You are from Ruleville all right," and he used a curse word, and he said, "We are going to make you wish you was dead."

I was carried out of that cell into another cell where they had two Negro prisoners. The State Highway Patrolman ordered the first Negro to take the blackjack. The first Negro prisoner ordered me, by orders from the State Highway Patrolman for me, to lay down on a bunk bed on my face, and I laid on my face. The first Negro began to beat, and I was beat by the first Negro until he was exhausted, and I was holding my hands behind me at that time on my left side because I suffered from polio when I was six years old. After the first Negro had beat until he was exhausted, the State Highway Patrolman ordered the second Negro to take the blackjack.

The second Negro began to beat and I began to work my feet, and the State Highway Patrolman ordered the first Negro who had beat to set on my feet to keep me from working my feet. I began to scream and one white man got up and began to beat me in my head and tell me to hush. One white man—my dress had worked up high, he walked over and pulled my dress down—and he pulled my dress back, back up.

I was in jail when Medgar Evers was murdered. . . .

All of this is on account we want to register, to become first-class citizens, and if the Freedom Democratic Party is not seated now, I question America, is this America, the land of the free and the home of the brave where we have to sleep with our telephones off the hooks because our lives be threatened daily because we want to live as decent human beings, in America?

Thank you.

Document 5: Malcolm X's speech, "The Ballot or the Bullet"

Malcolm X, the voice of dissatisfied urban blacks in the 1960s, was often the center of controversy for his radical ideas and his outspokenness. He spoke out against racism and criticized not only white society and the U.S. government, but also mainstream civil rights leaders. He delivered his "The Ballot or the Bullet" speech on April 3, 1964, as part of a seminar on the future of race relations in America. This speech, considered one of his best, explains his views on black nationalism and what American blacks should do to achieve equality. Central to his message, as always, were racial pride and brotherhood among African Americans.

The political philosophy of black nationalism means that the black man should control the politics and the politicians in his own community; no more. The black man in the black community has to be reeducated into the science of politics so he will know what politis is supposed to bring him in return. Don't be throwing out any ballots. A ballot is like a bullet. You don't throw your ballots until you see a target, and if that target is not within your reach, keep your ballot in your pocket. The political philosophy of black nationalism is being taught in the Christian church. It's being taught in the N.A.A.C.P. It's being taught in S.N.C.C. meetings. It's being taught in Muslim meetings. It's being taught where nothing but atheists and agnostics come together. It's being taught everywhere. Black people are fed up with the dillydallying, pussyfooting, compromising approach that we've been using toward getting our freedom. We want freedom *now*, but we're not going to get it saying "We Shall Overcome." We've got to fight until we overcome....

So I say, in spreading a gospel such as black nationalism, it is not designed to make the black man reevaluate the white man—you know him already—but to make the black man reevaluate himself. Don't change the white man's mind; you can't change his mind. And that whole thing about appealing to the moral conscience of America—America's conscience is bankrupt. She lost all conscience a long time ago. Uncle Sam has no conscience. They don't know what morals are. They don't try and eliminate an evil because it's evil, or because it's illegal, or because it's immoral; they eliminate it only when it threatens their existence. So you're wasting your time appealing to the moral conscience of a bankrupt man like Uncle Sam. If he had a conscience, he'd straighten this thing out with no more pressure being put upon him. So it is not necessary to change the white man's mind. We have to change our own mind. You can't change his mind about us. We've got to change our own minds about each other. We have to see each other with new eyes. We have to see each other as brothers and sisters. We have to come together with warmth so we can develop unity and harmony that's necessary to get this problem solved ourselves.

Copyright (c) 1965, 1989 by Betty Shabazz and Pathfinder Press. Reprinted with permission.

Source Notes

Chapter 1: Compromise and Economic Well-Being
1. Henry Steele Commager, *The Struggle for Racial Equality: A Documentary Record*. New York: Harper & Row, 1967, pp. viii–ix.
2. Milton Meltzer, ed., *The Black Americans: A History in Their Own Words, 1619–1983*. New York: HarperCollins, 1984, p. 136.
3. Booker T. Washington, *Up from Slavery*. New York: Doubleday, 1901, p. 37.
4. Washington, *Up from Slavery*, p. 51.
5. Washington, *Up from Slavery*, p. 61.
6. Quoted in Francis L. Broderick and August Meier, eds., *Negro Protest Thought in the Twentieth Century*. Indianapolis: Bobbs-Merrill, 1965, p. 13.
7. Quoted in Broderick and Meier, eds., *Negro Protest Thought in the Twentieth Century*, p. 13.
8. Quoted in Broderick and Meier, eds., *Negro Protest Thought in the Twentieth Century*, p. 16.
9. Quoted in Daniel J. O'Neill, ed., *Speeches by Black Americans*. Encino, CA: Dickenson, 1971, p. 81.
10. Quoted in Diana Wells, ed., *We Have a Dream: African-American Visions of Freedom*. New York: Carroll & Graf, 1993, pp. 123–24.
11. Quoted in Wells, ed., *We Have a Dream: African-American Visions of Freedom*, p. 124.
12. Quoted in Broderick and Meier, eds., *Negro Protest Thought in the Twentieth Century*, p. 7.
13. Quoted in Louis R. Harlan, Stuart B. Kaufman, Barbara S. Kraft, and Raymond W. Smock, eds., *The Booker T. Washington Papers*, Vol. 4 (1895–98). Urbana, IL: University of Illinois Press, 1975, p. 9.
14. Quoted in Hugh Hawkins, ed., *Booker T. Washington and His Critics: The Problem of Negro Leadership*. Boston: D. C. Heath, 1962, p. 22.
15. Quoted in Broderick and Meier, eds., *Negro Protest Thought in the Twentieth Century*, pp. 27–28.
16. Thomas E. Harris, *Analysis of the Clash over the Issues Between Booker T. Washington and W. E. B. Du Bois*. New York: Garland, 1993, p. 69.
17. Quoted in Hawkins, ed., *Booker T. Washington and His Critics: The Problem of Negro Leadership*, p. xiii.

Chapter 2: The Legal Battle for Civil Rights
18. Peter Irons, *A People's History of the Supreme Court: The Men and Women Whose Cases and Decisions Have Shaped Our Constitution*. New York: Penguin, 1999, p. 398.

19. Quoted in Mark V. Tushnet, *The NAACP's Legal Strategy Against Segregated Education, 1925–1950*. Chapel Hill, NC: University of North Carolina Press, 1987, p. 12.
20. Quoted in Richard Kluger, *Simple Justice: The History of* Brown v. Board of Education *and Black America's Struggle for Equality*. New York: Random House, 1975, p. 132.
21. Kluger, *Simple Justice: The History of* Brown v. Board of Education *and Black America's Struggle for Equality*, p. 134.
22. Quoted in Tushnet, *The NAACP's Legal Strategy Against Segregated Education, 1925–1950*, p. 34.
23. Irons, *A People's History of the Supreme Court: The Men and Women Whose Cases and Decisions Have Shaped Our Constitution*, p. 371.
24. Irons, *A People's History of the Supreme Court: The Men and Women Whose Cases and Decisions Have Shaped Our Constitution*, p. 386; James Haskins, *Thurgood Marshall: A Life for Justice*. New York: Henry Holt, 1992, pp. 89–90.
25. Irons, *A People's History of the Supreme Court: The Men and Women Whose Cases and Decisions Have Shaped Our Constitution*, p. 386.
26. Juan Williams, *Thurgood Marshall: American Revolutionary*. New York: Times Books, 1998, p. 216.
27. Quoted in Haskins, *Thurgood Marshall: A Life for Justice*, p. 93.
28. Quoted in Carl T. Rowan, *Dream Makers, Dream Breakers: The World of Justice Thurgood Marshall*. Boston: Little, Brown, 1993, p. 200.
29. Quoted in A. Craig Baird, ed., *Representative American Speeches: 1953–1954*. New York: H. W. Wilson, 1954, pp. 120–21.
30. Quoted in Michael D. Davis and Hunter C. Clark, *Thurgood Marshall: Warrior at the Bar, Rebel on the Bench*. New York: Carol, 1992, p. 177.
31. Irons, *A People's History of the Supreme Court: The Men and Women Whose Cases and Decisions Have Shaped Our Constitution*, p. 398.
32. Kermit L. Hall, James W. Ely, Jr., Joel B. Grossman, and William M. Wiecek, eds., *The Oxford Companion to the Supreme Court of the United States*. New York: Oxford University Press, 1992, p. 95.
33. Quoted in Hans P. Guth and Renee V. Hausmann, eds., *Essay: Reading with the Writer's Eye*. Belmont, CA: Wadsworth, 1984, p. 434.

Chapter 3: Nonviolence as a Weapon for Civil Rights

34. Quoted in James H. Cone, *Martin & Malcolm & America: A Dream or a Nightmare*. Maryknoll, NY: Orbis, 1991, pp. 23–24.

35. Quoted in Cone, *Martin & Malcolm & America: A Dream or a Nightmare*, pp. 66–67.
36. Quoted in Martin Luther King Jr., and Alex Ayers, ed., *The Wisdom of Martin Luther King, Jr.* Cleveland: Meridian, 1993, p. 92.
37. Quoted in King and Ayers, ed., *The Wisdom of Martin Luther King, Jr.*, p. 165.
38. Quoted in Kenneth R. Johnston, ed., *The Rhetoric of Conflict*. Indianapolis: Bobbs-Merrill, 1969, pp. 34–35.
39. Quoted in Johnston, ed., *The Rhetoric of Conflict*, p. 35.
40. Cone, *Martin & Malcolm & America: A Dream or a Nightmare*, pp. 140–41.
41. Quoted in Andrew Carroll, ed., *Letters of a Nation: A Collection of Extraordinary American Letters*. New York: Kodansha International, 1997, p. 209.
42. Quoted in Johnston, ed., *The Rhetoric of Conflict*, p. 36.
43. Quoted in Carroll, ed., *Letters of a Nation: A Collection of Extraordinary American Letters*, p. 211.
44. Quoted in Johnston, ed., *The Rhetoric of Conflict*, pp. 36–37.
45. Quoted in Johnston, ed., *The Rhetoric of Conflict*, p. 37.
46. Quoted in Johnston, ed., *The Rhetoric of Conflict*, p. 39.
47. Martin Luther King Jr., *Why We Can't Wait*. New York: Harper & Row, 1963, pp. 105–106.
48. Taylor Branch, *Parting the Waters: America in the King Years, 1954–1963*. New York: Simon & Schuster, 1988, p. 744.
49. Quoted in Theodore C. Sorensen, ed., *"Let Every Word Go Forth": The Speeches, Statements, and Writings of John F. Kennedy 1947–1963*. New York: Bantam Doubleday Dell, 1988, p. 194.
50. Quoted in King and Ayers, ed., *The Wisdom of Martin Luther King, Jr.*, pp. 266–67.

Chapter 4: The Fight for a Political Voice

51. Quoted in *The World Almanac and Book of Facts 2000*. Mahwah, NJ: Primedia Reference, 1999, p. 545.
52. Quoted in Meltzer, ed., *The Black Americans: A History in Their Own Words*, pp. 150–51.
53. Quoted in Jeffrey C. Stewart, *1001 Things Everyone Should Know about African American History*. New York: Bantam Doubleday Dell, 1996, p. 130.
54. Quoted in Meltzer, ed., *The Black Americans: A History in Their Own Words*, pp. 186–87.
55. Quoted in Kay Mills, *This Little Light of Mine: The Life of Fannie Lou Hamer*. New York: Plume (Penguin), 1993, p. 24.

56. Eric R. Burner, *And Gently He Led Them: Robert Parris Moses and Civil Rights in Mississippi*. New York: New York University Press, 1994, p. 6.
57. Burner, *And Gently He Led Them: Robert Parris Moses and Civil Rights in Mississippi*, p. 22.
58. Quoted in Chana Kai Lee, *For Freedom's Sake: The Life of Fannie Lou Hamer*. Urbana & Chicago: University of Illinois Press, 1999, p. 26.
59. Lee, *For Freedom's Sake: The Life of Fannie Lou Hamer*, p. 26.
60. Lee, *For Freedom's Sake: The Life of Fannie Lou Hamer*, p. 69.
61. John Dittmer, *Local People: The Struggle for Civil Rights in Mississippi*. Urbana, IL: University of Illinois Press, 1994, p. 288.
62. Quoted in Mills, *This Little Light of Mine: The Life of Fannie Lou Hamer*, pp. 120–21.
63. Quoted in Lee, *For Freedom's Sake: The Life of Fannie Lou Hamer*, p. 89.
64. Tracy Sugarman, *Stranger at the Gates: A Summer in Mississippi*. New York: Hill and Wang, 1966, pp. 195–96.
65. Quoted in Lee, *For Freedom's Sake: The Life of Fannie Lou Hamer*, pp. 96, 99.
66. Quoted in Mills, *This Little Light of Mine: The Life of Fannie Lou Hamer*, p. 311.
67. Quoted in Mills, *This Little Light of Mine: The Life of Fannie Lou Hamer*, p. 311.

Chapter 5: Rejection of Integration
68. Quoted in Cone, *Martin & Malcolm & America: A Dream or a Nightmare*, p. 13.
69. Cone, *Martin & Malcolm & America: A Dream or a Nightmare*, pp. 14–15.
70. Quoted in Bruce Perry, ed., *Malcolm X: The Last Speeches*. New York: Betty Shabazz, Bruce Perry, and Pathfinder Press, 1989, p. 192.
71. Quoted in Columbus Salley, *The Black 100: A Ranking of the Most Influential African-Americans, Past and Present*. New York: Citadel, 1993, pp. 91–92.
72. Quoted in Kenneth B. Clark, *The Negro Protest: James Baldwin, Malcolm X, and Martin Luther King Talk with Kenneth B. Clark*. Boston: Beacon, 1963, pp. 25–26.
73. Quoted in Cone, *Martin & Malcolm & America: A Dream or a Nightmare*, p. 113.
74. George Breitman, ed., *Malcolm X Speaks: Selected Speeches and Statements*. New York: Pathfinder Press and Betty Shabazz, 1965, 1989, p. 51.
75. Quoted in James Haskins, *Profiles in Black Power*. New York: Doubleday, 1972, p. 116.

76. Quoted in Cone, *Martin & Malcolm & America: A Dream or a Nightmare*, p. 193.
77. Quoted in Philip S. Foner, ed., *The Voice of Black America: Major Speeches by Negroes in the United States, 1797–1971*. New York: Simon & Schuster, 1972, pp. 986–87.
78. Quoted in Foner, ed., *The Voice of Black America: Major Speeches by Negroes in the United States, 1797–1971*, p. 987.
79. Quoted in Foner, ed., *The Voice of Black America: Major Speeches by Negroes in the United States, 1797–1971*, pp. 987–88.
80. Quoted in Foner, ed., *The Voice of Black America: Major Speeches by Negroes in the United States, 1797–1971*, p. 992.
81. Quoted in Foner, ed., *The Voice of Black America: Major Speeches by Negroes in the United States, 1797–1971*, p. 993.
82. Quoted in Foner, ed., *The Voice of Black America: Major Speeches by Negroes in the United States, 1797–1971*, p. 1000.
83. Quoted in Perry, ed., *Malcolm X: The Last Speeches*, p. 14.
84. Quoted in Cone, *Martin & Malcolm & America: A Dream or a Nightmare*, pp. 39–40.
85. Cone, *Martin & Malcolm & America: A Dream or a Nightmare*, pp. 291–92.
86. Quoted in Perry, ed., *Malcolm X: The Last Speeches*, p. 19.

For Further Reading

Zita Allen, *Black Women Leaders of the Civil Rights Movement*. Danbury, CT: Franklin Watts, 1996. A study of the role that women, largely unknown and behind the scenes, played in the movement. It is as much about the struggle for gender equality as for racial equality.

Jules Archer, *They Had a Dream: The Civil Rights Struggle from Frederick Douglass to Marcus Garvey to Martin Luther King and Malcolm X*. New York: Puffin, 1996. Biographies of the four civil rights activists, combined with historical perspectives, interviews with well-known activists, and essays. Well-written, well-researched, illustrated with black-and-white photographs. Also contains a bibliography. An excellent resource.

Sara Bullard, *Free at Last: A History of the Civil Rights Movement and Those Who Died in the Struggle*. New York: Oxford University Press, 1993. A chronological study of the civil rights movement. The last section contains biographical sketches of forty people, both black and white, who were part of the movement. Also contains a bibliography.

Kerry Candaele et al., eds., *Bound for Glory: From the Great Migration to the Harlem Renaissance, 1910–1930*. New York: Chelsea House, 1997. A definitive study of African American history in the early twentieth century. It focuses on the black migration from the South to the industrial cities of the North and features the contributions of Louis Armstrong, Satchel Paige, Marcus Garvey, and Langston Hughes.

Ed Clayton, *Martin Luther King: The Peaceful Warrior*, edited by Pat MacDonald. New York: Archway, 1996. A popular biography of Martin Luther King Jr., which introduces young readers to his philosophy and achievements. Attractively illustrated and readable.

Kathryn T. Cryan-Hicks, *W. E. B. DuBois: Crusader for Peace*. Carlisle, MA: Discovery Enterprises, 1991. A simple, readable biography of the sociologist, educator, and civil rights activist. Well-illustrated.

Mark Davies, *Malcolm X: Another Side of the Movement*. Englewood Cliffs, NJ: Silver Burdett, 1990. A simple biography of the African American activist.

Mark E. Dudley, Brown v. Board of Education: *School Desegregation*. Brookfield, CT: Twenty First Century Books, 1995. Background, personalities, and court deliberations involved in the case that outlawed school segregation in the United States.

Charles George, *Life Under the Jim Crow Laws*. San Diego: Lucent Books, 2000. A well-researched, comprehensive, clearly written history of the Jim Crow era, from Reconstruction to the 1960s. Chapters cover discrimination in daily life, schools, the workplace, and the courts. Contains footnotes, a bibliography, and an index.

Linda and Charles George, *Civil Rights Marches*. Danbury, CT: Children's Press, 1999. A readable, well-researched account of Martin Luther King's nonviolent protest movement in the United States, focusing on the most famous marches—Montgomery, the Prayer Pilgrimage, Birmingham, the March on Washington, and Selma. Also includes background on the philosophy behind the movement. Contains a glossary, a time line, and an index.

Scott Gillam, *Discrimination: Prejudice in Action*. Springfield, NJ: Enslow, 1995. A history of discrimination and ways of dealing with it.

Michael Golay, *Reconstruction and Reaction: The Emancipation of the Slaves, 1861–1913*. New York: Facts On File, 1996. An anthology of documents associated with African American achievements during and after Reconstruction.

Joy Hakim, *An Age of Extremes*. New York: Oxford University Press, 1994. Part of a well-written, well-organized, and well-illustrated history of the United States. This volume covers the period between 1880 and World War I.

Joyce Hansen, *Women of Hope: African-Americans Who Made a Difference*. New York: Scholastic, 1998. Twelve short biographies of famous African American women, including Fannie Lou Hamer. Contains stunning black-and-white photographs, a list of other famous women, and a bibliography.

James Haskins, *Separate, but Not Equal: The Dream and the Struggle*. New York: Scholastic, 1998. Background on the history of African Americans' struggle for equal rights in education, from slavery to affirmative action. Landmark court cases are discussed in detail, as well as the philosophies of W. E. B. Du Bois and Booker T. Washington. Contains few illustrations but a wealth of facts and statistics, as well as a bibliography and an index.

Debra Hess, *Thurgood Marshall: The Fight for Equal Justice*. Englewood Cliffs, NJ: Silver Burdett, 1990. A biography of Marshall, focusing on his landmark Supreme Court case for the NAACP and his later appointment to the Court.

Stuart A. Kallen, *The Twentieth Century and the Harlem Renaissance: A History of Black People in America, 1880–1930*. Edina, MN: Abdo and Daughters, 1990. Black history in the early decades of the twentieth century. Includes profiles of W. E. B. Du Bois, Booker T. Washington, Langston Hughes, and Louis Armstrong.

Deborah Kent, *Thurgood Marshall: The Fight for Equal Justice*. Danbury, CT: Children's Press, 1997. A clear, simple text about the legal leader of the NAACP and later Supreme Court justice. Contains many photographs and a time line.

Pat McKissack et al., *The Civil Rights Movement in America: From 1865 to the Present*. Danbury, CT: Children's Press, 1991. Traces the black struggle from Reconstruction to the present, comparing African Americans' struggle with that of other minorities.

Christopher Martin, *Mohandas Gandhi*. Minneapolis: Lerner, 2000. Biography of the leader of India's independence movement and one of the philosophical inspirations for the nonviolent American civil rights movement.

Zak Mettger, *Reconstuction: America After the Civil War*. New York: Lodestar, 1994. A well-written account, using historical documents and firsthand accounts of former slaves and slave owners. It emphasizes the legislative maneuvering of Southern states to deny blacks their civil rights. Contains clear, concise explanations, many illustrations, a glossary, and a bibliography.

Walter Dean Myers, *Malcolm X: By Any Means Necessary*. New York: Scholastic, 1998. An award-winning biography of this controversial figure in African American history. Includes historical background about the civil rights movement.

Fred Powledge, *We Shall Overcome: Heroes of the Civil Rights Movement*. New York: Scribner, 1993. Presents the personal experiences of ten "ordinary" civil rights workers. Well organized and passionate, it gives the reader insights into what the movement was really like.

Mark Rowh, *W. E. B. Du Bois: Champion of Civil Rights*. Berkeley Heights, NJ: Enslow, 1999. Biography of Du Bois, including his opposition to Booker T. Washington and his role in the establishment of the Niagara Movement and the NAACP.

David Rubel et al., *Fannie Lou Hamer: From Sharecropping to Politics*. Englewood Cliffs, NJ: Silver Burdett, 1990. Biography of the poor sharecropper who inspired thousands in Mississippi's voter registration drives of the 1960s.

Michael Weber, *The African American Civil Rights Movement*. San Diego: Lucent Books, 1998. An overview of the movement, focusing on the causes and consequences.

Works Consulted

Herbert Aptheker, ed., *A Documentary History of the Negro People in the United States, Vol. 2: From the Reconstruction Era to 1910*. New York: Citadel, 1951. One volume in a series of collections of speeches, letters, articles, laws, and so forth, produced by African Americans. Fully indexed.

———, ed., *A Documentary History of the Negro People in the United States 1960–1968, Vol. 7: From the Alabama Protests to the Death of Martin Luther King, Jr*. New York: Citadel, 1994. One volume in a series of collections of speeches, letters, articles, laws, and so forth, produced by African Americans. Fully indexed.

A. Craig Baird, ed., *Representative American Speeches: 1953–1954*. New York: H. W. Wilson, 1954. One volume of an ongoing series recording significant American speeches given by politicians, statesmen, celebrities, scientists, and others.

Howard Ball, *A Defiant Life: Thurgood Marshall and the Persistence of Racism in America*. New York: Crown, 1998. A thorough, well-researched biography of Marshall and the NAACP's struggle for racial equality in the United States. Fully indexed.

Jim Bishop, *The Days of Martin Luther King, Jr*. New York: Putnam, 1971. One of the most exhaustive biographies of King ever written. Fully indexed.

Randall Bland, *Private Pressure on Public Law: The Legal Career of Thurgood Marshall*. Port Washington, NY: Kennikat, 1973. A concise, fully indexed biography of Marshall's legal career, from law school to the Supreme Court.

Taylor Branch, *Parting the Waters: America in the King Years, 1954–1963*. New York: Simon & Schuster, 1988. A stunning portrait of King's rise to greatness, illuminating both the public and the private man. Winner of the 1989 Pulitzer Prize for History and the National Book Critics Circle Award. Fully indexed and footnoted, with an extensive bibliography.

George Breitman, ed., *Malcolm X Speaks: Selected Speeches and Statements*. New York: Pathfinder Press and Betty Shabazz, 1965, 1989. A collection of speeches, with commentary.

Francis L. Broderick and August Meier, eds., *Negro Protest Thought in the Twentieth Century*. Indianapolis: Bobbs-Merrill, 1965. An anthology of statements, speeches, letters, articles, and so forth, along with commentary, dealing with blacks' struggle for equality. Fully indexed.

Eric R. Burner, *And Gently He Led Them: Robert Parris Moses and Civil Rights in Mississippi*. New York: New York University Press, 1994. An easy-to-read biography of Moses and his work in the civil rights movement in Mississippi. Fully indexed.

Andrew Carroll, ed., *Letters of a Nation: A Collection of Extraordinary American Letters*. New York: Kodansha International, 1997. An extensive collection of letters and notes written by or to famous or not-so-famous people, from the beginnings of the United States to the present day. Fully indexed.

Kenneth B. Clark, *The Negro Protest: James Baldwin, Malcolm X, and Martin Luther King Talk with Kenneth B. Clark*. Boston: Beacon, 1963. One of the key participants in the *Brown v. Board of Education* case, Clark writes a scholarly psychological study of three famous African Americans, based on interviews that he conducted with each of them about their image of themselves, their views on the successes and failures of the civil rights movement, and their predictions of the future of race relations in the United States.

Henry Steele Commager, ed., *Documents of American History, Vol. I (To 1898)*. New York: Appleton-Century-Crofts, 1968. An anthology of famous American documents from 1492 to 1898. Fully indexed.

———, ed., *The Struggle for Racial Equality: A Documentary Record*. New York: Harper & Row, 1967. An anthology of documents pertaining to African Americans' fight for equal rights, from the beginnings of slavery through the years of the civil rights movement. Fully indexed.

James H. Cone, *Martin & Malcolm & America: A Dream or a Nightmare*. Maryknoll, NY: Orbis, 1991. An extensive, well-researched comparison and contrast of King and Malcolm X and their views of America. An in-depth analysis of these two complex individuals and their philosophies. Fully indexed.

The Congressional Record–House, Sept. 17, 1965, pp. 24268–24269. The day-to-day record of testimony in the House of Representatives.

Charles P. Cozic, ed., *Civil Liberties: Opposing Viewpoints*. San Diego: Greenhaven Press, 1994. An extensive debate, packed with arguments, speeches, and articles supporting both sides of each issue. Includes useful editorial overviews and commentaries, as well as complete footnotes and a bibliography.

Kenneth C. Davis, *Don't Know Much About History: Everything You Need to Know About American History but Never Learned*. New York: Avon, 1990. A humorous yet highly informative compilation of facts and anecdotes from American history—from the arrival of Columbus to the Iran-contra affair. It explodes long-held myths and misconceptions and is a handy reference book. Fully indexed.

Michael D. Davis and Hunter R. Clark, *Thurgood Marshall: Warrior at the Bar, Rebel on the Bench*. New York: Carol, 1992. A well-written, extensively researched biography of Marshall, from birth through law school to the Supreme Court and beyond. Fully indexed.

Randall E. Decker, ed., *Patterns of Exposition*. Boston: Little, Brown, 1966. An anthology of essays, articles, and speeches relating to a wide range of topics. A standard college text. Indexed by topic, style, and author.

Jerry DeMuth, "Tired of Being Sick and Tired," *The Nation*, June 1, 1964. A magazine article based on an interview with Fannie Lou Hamer during her run for political office in Mississippi in 1964.

John Dittmer, *Local People: The Struggle for Civil Rights in Mississippi*. Urbana, IL: University of Illinois Press, 1994. A well-researched analysis of the civil rights struggle in Mississippi. Includes biographical information about people involved, both locals and outsiders. Fully indexed.

Alice Moore Dunbar, ed., *Masterpieces of Negro Eloquence: The Best Speeches Delivered by the Negro from the Days of Slavery to the Present Time*. New York: G. K. Hall, 1997. An anthology of speeches by famous African Americans, along with commentary and analysis. Fully indexed.

The Editors of Time-Life Books, eds. *Perseverance: African American Voices of Triumph*. Alexandria, VA: Time-Life Books, 1993. One volume of a series on the history and culture of African Americans from slavery to the present day. Fully indexed and lavishly illustrated.

Philip S. Foner, ed., *The Voice of Black America: Major Speeches by Negoes in the United States, 1797–1971*. New York: Simon & Schuster, 1972. An anthology of famous speeches by African Americans. Fully indexed.

Philip S. Foner and Robert James Branham, eds., *Lift Every Voice: African American Oratory 1787–1900*. Tuscaloosa, AL, and London: University of Alabama Press, 1998. An updated and more complete anthology of famous speeches by African Americans. Includes analysis and commentary. Fully indexed.

David J. Garrow, *Bearing the Cross: Martin Luther King, Jr., and the Southern Christian Leadership Conference*. New York: William Morrow & Co., 1986. A Pulitzer Prize–winning biography of King, based on more than seven hundred interviews, King's personal papers, and thousands of FBI documents. One of the most comprehensive books ever written about King, by the senior advisor for *Eyes on the Prize*, the award-winning PBS television documentary history of the American civil rights movement. Contains ninety pages of footnotes, an unbelievable bibliography, and a meticulous index.

Paula Giddings, *When and Where I Enter: The Impact of Black Women on Race and Sex in America*. New York: William Morrow, Inc., 1984. A landmark appraisal of black women's unsung contributions to the struggles for racial and sexual equality, using speeches, diaries, and letters of influential black women.

Peter Goldman, *The Death and Life of Malcolm X*. New York: Harper & Row, 1973. A well-written, thoroughly researched biography. Fully indexed.

Hans P. Guth and Renee V. Hausmann, *Essay: Reading with the Writer's Eye*. Belmont, CA: Wadsworth, 1984. An anthology of essays dealing with a variety of topics. Fully indexed.

David Halberstam, *The Children*. New York: Random House, 1998. An in-depth study of the young black people involved in civil rights protests in Nashville, Tennessee, in 1960, by the Pulitzer Prize–winning *New York Times* reporter and author. At the time of the demonstrations, he was the principal reporter for *The Nashville Tennessean* and witnessed the events personally. Contains footnotes, a bibliography, and an index.

Kermit L. Hall, James W. Ely Jr., Joel B. Grossman, and William M. Wiecek, eds., *The Oxford Companion to the Supreme Court of the United States*. New York: Oxford University Press, 1992. An incredibly complete and up-to-date encyclopedia of information about the Court, containing a dictionary of cases, biographies of justices, clerks, lawyers, and others, an explanation of Court procedures and terms, and a mountain of other data. Both useful to the expert and interesting to the layman. Contains both a case index and a topical index. An extremely useful source.

Walter Harding, *A Thoreau Handbook*. New York: New York University Press, 1959. An analysis of and a commentary on Thoreau's writings and philosophy, along with biographical information. Contains footnotes, a bibliography, and an index.

Walter Harding, George Brenner, and Paul A. Doyle, eds., *Henry David Thoreau: Studies and Commentaries*. Rutherford, NJ: Fairleigh Dickinson University Press, 1972. An extensive study of the man and his works. A scholarly analysis of Thoreau's ideas. Contains footnotes, a bibliography, and an index.

Louis R. Harlan and John W. Blassingame, eds., *The Booker T. Washington Papers, Vol. 1 (The Autobiographical Writings)*. Urbana, IL: University of Illinois Press, 1972. One volume of an extensive collection of Washington's personal and professional papers—letters, notes, speeches, articles, and so forth. Fully footnoted and indexed.

Louis R. Harlan, Stuart B. Kaufman, and Raymond W. Smock, eds., *The Booker T. Washington Papers, Vol. 3 (1889–95)*. Urbana, IL: University of Illinois Press, 1974. One volume of an extensive collection of Washington's personal and professional papers—letters, notes, speeches, articles, and so forth. Fully footnoted and indexed.

Louis R. Harlan, Stuart B. Kaufman, Barbara S. Kraft, and Raymond W. Smock, eds., *The Booker T. Washington Papers, Vol. 4 (1895–98)*. Urbana, IL: University of Illinois Press, 1975. One volume of an extensive collection of Washington's personal and professional papers—letters, notes, speeches, articles, and so forth. Fully footnoted and indexed.

Janet Harris, *The Long Freedom Road: The Civil Rights Story*. New York: McGraw-Hill, 1967. A readable overview of the civil rights struggle.

Thomas E. Harris, *Analysis of the Clash over the Issues Between Booker T. Washington and W. E. B. Du Bois*. New York: Garland, 1993. A scholarly study of the differences and similarities between two great African Americans at the turn of the century, based on their letters, speeches, articles, and opinions shared with others. Contains extensive analysis and commentary, tons of footnotes, and a complete index.

Maureen Harrison and Steve Gilbert, eds., *Landmark Decisions of the United States Supreme Court*. Beverly Hills, CA: Excellent Books, 1991. A comprehensive collection of information and commentary about key Supreme Court decisions and the people involved. Contains footnotes and an index.

James Haskins, *Profiles in Black Power*. Garden City, NY: Doubleday, 1972. A comprehensive study of black militants in the 1960s, including extensive biographical and philosophical information about Malcolm X, as well as historical background on the black nationalist movement.

———, *Thurgood Marshall: A Life for Justice*. New York: Henry Holt, 1992. An excellent, easy-to-read biography of Marshall from his childhood to his retirement from the Supreme Court. Fully indexed.

Hugh Hawkins, ed., *Booker T. Washington and His Critics: The Problem of Negro Leadership*. Boston: D. C. Heath, 1962. A scholarly analysis of Washington's philosophy and programs and those who disagreed with him. Footnoted and fully indexed.

Peter Irons, *A People's History of the Supreme Court: The Men and Women Whose Cases and Decisions Have Shaped Our Constitution*. New York: Penguin, 1999. A unique study of the Supreme Court and its most important cases, written more about the individuals involved in the cases—the defendants and lawyers—than about the verdicts or the justices. Very fascinating reading for legal scholars or ordinary citizens. Contains extensive footnotes and an index.

Kenneth R. Johnston, ed., *The Rhetoric of Conflict*. Indianapolis: Bobbs-Merrill, 1969. An anthology of famous speeches, articles, and letters written by people in conflict. Includes extensive commentary and analysis of the style and the underlying philosophy involved in the documents.

Martin Luther King Jr., *Letter from Birmingham Jail*. New York: HarperCollins, 1994. A reprint of King's famous letter, with commentary.

———, *Why We Can't Wait*. New York: Harper & Row, 1963. One of King's most important books, detailing the philosophy behind the movement and the events of the Birmingham campaign, including the full text of the "Letter from Birmingham Jail."

Martin Luther King Jr., and Alex Ayres, eds., *The Wisdom of Martin Luther King, Jr*. Cleveland: Meridian, 1993. An accessible anthology of statements King made on a variety of subjects. Taken from speeches, books, letters, and articles, the phrases and sentences are organized by topic. Quite useful for a student of King.

Richard Kluger, *Simple Justice: The History of Brown v. Board of Education and Black America's Struggle for Equality*. New York: Random House, 1975. An exhaustive study of the *Brown* case and how it related to the overall struggle for equality. Extensively footnoted and fully indexed.

Chana Kai Lee, *For Freedom's Sake: The Life of Fannie Lou Hamer*. Urbana and Chicago: University of Illinois Press, 1999. An easy-to-read biography of Hamer, from childhood to sharecropping to political activism and public service. Fully indexed.

Peter B. Levy, *The Civil Rights Movement*. Westport, CT: Greenwood, 1998. A wonderfully useful guide to the civil rights movement, including concise biographies of key individuals, an anthology of primary documents dealing with the movement in the years 1947 through 1969, a glossary of terms and organizations, and a comprehensive annotated bibliography. Fully indexed.

Leon F. Litwack, *Trouble in Mind: Black Southerners in the Age of Jim Crow*. New York: Knopf, 1998. The definitive source on the Jim Crow era. The Pulitzer Prize–winning historian draws on a vast array of contemporary documents and first-person narratives from both blacks and whites. Contains hundreds of footnotes, an incredible bibliography, and an extensive index.

Malcolm X and Alex Haley, *The Autobiography of Malcolm X*. New York: Ballantine Books, 1964. The definitive story of Malcolm X, told through a lengthy series of interviews with the award-winning author of *Roots*. Written in an easy, conversational style.

Milton Meltzer, ed., *The Black Americans: A History in Their Own Words, 1916–1983*. New York: HarperCollins, 1984. An anthology of writings by black Americans, from slave diaries to participants in the civil rights movement. Includes commentary and background information about events and personalities. Fully indexed.

———, ed., *In Their Own Words: A History of the American Negro 1916–1966*. New York: Thomas Y. Crowell, 1967. An anthology of writings by famous African Americans, with commentary and analysis. Fully indexed.

Kay Mills, *This Little Light of Mine: The Life of Fannie Lou Hamer*. New York: Plume (Penguin), 1993. A thorough, sensitive biography chronicling the civil rights movement in Mississippi and the strength and determination of one uncommon woman. Contains extensive footnotes and time line. Fully indexed.

Nicolaus Mills, *Like a Holy Crusade: Mississippi 1964—The Turning of the Civil Rights Movement in America*. Chicago: Ivan R. Dee, 1992. The history of the Mississippi Summer Project of 1964, from its origin to its aftermath. Discusses the consequences of this crucial period in the civil rights movement, both victories and tragedies.

Constance Baker Motley, *Equal Justice Under Law: An Autobiography*. New York: Farrar, Straus and Giroux, 1998. Personal memoir of one of the NAACP Legal Defense Fund team. Includes many personal insights and behind-the-scenes anecdotes. Fully indexed.

Daniel J. O'Neill, ed., *Speechs by Black Americans*. Encino, CA: Dickenson, 1971. An anthology of African American speeches, with commentary and analysis. Fully indexed.

Wayland Maxfield Parrish and Marie Hochmuth, eds., *American Speeches*. New York: Longmans, Green, 1954. An anthology of famous speeches covering a variety of topics.

Bruce Perry, *Malcolm: The Life of a Man Who Changed Black America*. Barrytown, NY: Station Hill, 1991. A well-researched biography. Fully indexed.

Bruce Perry, ed., *Malcolm X: The Last Speeches*. New York: Betty Shabazz, Bruce Perry, and Pathfinder Press, 1989. An anthology of speeches showing Malcolm X's transformation from a radical black militant to a more tolerant, open-minded activist after his pilgrimage to Mecca. Includes commentary.

Houston Peterson, *A Treasury of the World's Great Speeches*. New York: Simon & Schuster, 1954, 1965. An anthology of speeches by individuals around the world. Comprehensive, with footnotes and an index.

Jack Harrison Pollack, *Earl Warren: The Judge Who Changed America*. Englewood Cliffs, NJ: Prentice-Hall, 1979. An enjoyable biography about one of the most influential justices ever to sit on the Supreme Court. Fully footnoted and indexed.

Carl T. Rowan, *Dream Makers, Dream Breakers: The World of Justice Thurgood Marshall*. Boston: Little, Brown, 1993. An extensive, well-researched biography of Marshall and some of the individuals whom he dealt with. Contains footnotes and a bibliography. Fully indexed.

Columbus Salley, *The Black 100: A Ranking of the Most Influential African-Americans, Past and Present*. New York: Citadel, 1993. An anthology of short biographies and commentaries about the one hundred African Americans whom the author ranks as the most influential. An excellent resource with concise, accessible information. Fully indexed.

Arthur M. Schlesinger Jr., *A Thousand Days: John F. Kennedy in the White House*. New York: Crown, 1983. A comprehensive Pulitzer Prize–winning biography of Kennedy during his presidency, from campaign and election to assassination. Contains hundreds of footnotes, an extensive bibliography, and a full index.

Theodore C. Sorensen, ed., *"Let Every Word Go Forth": The Speeches, Statements, and Writings of John F. Kennedy 1947–1963*. New York: Bantam Doubleday Dell, 1988. An anthology of JFK's most important statements, organized by general topic. Includes a very useful commentary and analysis. Fully indexed.

Kenneth M. Stampp, *The Era of Reconstruction, 1865–1877*. New York: Vintage (Random House), 1965. A comprehensive study of the Reconstruction era, containing many personal accounts from both blacks and whites. Contains extensive bibliography. Fully indexed.

Jeffrey C. Stewart, *1001 Things Everyone Should Know About African American History*. New York: Bantam Doubleday Dell, 1996. A readable, interesting collection of facts and stories about African American history. This well-organized, concise book offers dozens of biographical sketches of important African Americans. Well illustrated, with a selected bibliography and a complete index.

Tracy Sugarman, *Stranger at the Gates: A Summer in Mississippi*. New York: Hill and Wang, 1966. Memoirs of a Northern journalist who came to the South during the Freedom Summer of 1964.

Mark V. Tushnet, *Making Civil Rights Law: Thurgood Marshall and the Supreme Court, 1936–1961*. New York: Oxford University Press, 1994. A scholarly study of the development of Marshall's legal philosophy, his most famous cases, and his judicial record on the Supreme Court. Fully footnoted and indexed.

———, *The NAACP's Legal Strategy Against Segregated Education, 1925–1950*. Chapel Hill, NC: University of North Carolina

Press, 1987. A thorough analysis of the NAACP's legal strategy in the education cases. Includes background information about people involved in the cases. Contains footnotes and a complete index.

Booker T. Washington, *Up from Slavery*. New York: Doubleday, 1901. The autobiography of the famous educator, statesman, and scholar. Includes a detailed chronology of Washington's life.

Carol Wekesser, ed., *Social Justice: Opposing Viewpoints*. San Diego: Greenhaven Press, 1990. An extensive debate, packed with arguments, speeches, and articles supporting both sides of each issue. Includes useful editorial overviews and commentaries, as well as complete footnotes and a bibliography.

Diana Wells, ed., *We Have a Dream: African-American Visions of Freedom*. New York: Carroll & Graf, 1993. An anthology of works (speeches, articles, excerpts, and essays) by black writers, centering on the struggle for civil rights.

Mark Whitman, *Removing a Badge of Slavery: The Record of* Brown v. Board of Education. Princeton, NJ, and New York: Markus Wiener, 1993. An in-depth study of the landmark Supreme Court case, from its inception to the final decision. Contains many footnotes.

Juan Williams, *Thurgood Marshall: American Revolutionary*. New York: Times Books, 1998. Probably the definitive biography of Marshall. Extensive research based on hundreds of interviews, Marshall's personal and judicial records, and Supreme Court records. Contains a comprehensive bibliography. Fully footnoted and indexed.

William J. Wolf, *Thoreau: Mystic, Prophet, Ecologist*. Philadelphia: United Church Press, 1974. A scholarly analysis of Thoreau, his philosophy, and his work. Extensively researched. Fully indexed.

Bob Woodward and Scott Armstrong, *The Brethren: Inside the Supreme Court*. New York: Simon & Schuster, 1979. A complete study of the Supreme Court, focusing on the men and women who have sat on the bench. Well researched. Fully footnoted and indexed.

C. Vann Woodward, *The Strange Career of Jim Crow*, 3d ed. New York: Oxford University Press, 1974. Probably the most widely quoted book on the subject, it offers a well-organized and in-depth treatment of the origins and practices of the Jim Crow system. Written by a Pulitzer Prize–winning historian.

The World Almanac and Book of Facts 2000. Mahwah, NJ: Primedia Reference, 1999. One of the most useful research tools available. Includes thousands of bits of information about every subject under the sun. Well organized, with an extensive index (in the front of the book). An easily affordable paperback, published annually.

Index

Abernathy, Ralph, 46, 60
ACLU. *See* American Civil Liberties Union
African American suffrage, 58
  see also black voting rights
Ali, Noble Drew, 74–75
American Civil Liberties Union (ACLU), 29
American Fund for Public Service. *See* Garland Fund
American Missionary Association, 14
Armstrong, Samuel Chapman, 14–15, 16
"Atlanta Compromise" speech. *See* Washington, Booker T.
Atlanta Exposition
  Booker T. Washington at, 12, 17–22
  inclusion of blacks in, 17

"The Ballot or the Bullet" speech. *See* Malcolm X
Bevel, James, 53, 61
Birmingham News (newspaper), 46
Birmingham protests, 42
  children's protest, 53
  Martin Luther King and
    arrest of, 46
    criticized by white clergymen, 46–48
    "Letter from Birmingham Jail," 48–53, 91–101
    plan for protests, 45–46
  national impact of, 54–55
  nonviolent commitment card, 48
  number of demonstrators arrested, 53
  success of, 54
black children
  children's protest in Birmingham, 53
  psychological effects of segregation, 32–34
black colleges and universities, 23
black nationalism
  Islam and, 74–75
  leaders in the early twentieth century, 74–75
  Malcolm X and, 72
    "The Ballot or the Bullet" speech, 79–83, 101–102
    criticism of mainstream civil rights movement and integration, 78–79
    in the Nation of Islam, 76, 77
    views on black pride, 77

  views on hate and militancy, 77–78
  militancy and, 72
  Nation of Islam and, 75–77
  origins of, 72–74
Black 100, The (Salley), 31
black schools
  created by the Freedmen's Bureau, 13, 14
  Hampton Normal and Industrial Institute, 14–15
  Tuskegee Institute, 16–17
  see also vocational training
Black Star Steamship Corporation, 74
black voting rights
  Booker T. Washington and, 59
  early supporters of, 58
  Fannie Lou Hamer and, 57–58, 63–65, 66–69
  Fifteenth Amendment and, 8, 57, 58
  restrictions on, 10–11
  Robert Parris Moses and, 61, 62–63
  voter registration drives in Mississippi, 57–58, 60–61, 62–63, 65
  W. E. B. Du Bois and, 59–60
Bolling v. Sharpe, 32
Branch, Taylor, 54
Briggs v. Elliott, 32
Brown v. the Board of Education of Topeka, Kansas
  arguments before the Supreme Court, 34–38
    text of Marshall's closing arguments, 89–91
  Charles Hamilton Houston and, 31
  court cases associated with, 32
  evidence on the psychological effects of segregation, 32–34
  legacy of, 41
  reluctant compliance by Southern states, 40
  Southern response to, 39–40
  Supreme Court decision in, 26, 38–39
Bullock, Rufus B., 22
Bureau of Refugees, Freedmen, and Abandoned Lands. *See* Freedmen's Bureau
Burner, Eric R., 62–63
Byrd, Harry, 40
Byrnes, James, 40

Camus, Albert, 62
Carnegie, Andrew, 22

Carter, Hodding, III, 70
Carter, Jimmy, 71
"Cast Down Your Bucket" speech. *See*
   Washington, Booker T.
   text of, 86–89
"Civil Disobedience" (Thoreau), 43
civil rights
   accommodationist views
      Booker T. Washington's advocacy of, 12, 13, 18–22
      criticism of, 22–24
      legacy of, 25
   legal strategies in
      basis of, 26–27
      Brown v. the Board of Education, 26, 32–41
      challenges to segregation in higher education, 30, 32
      Charles Hamilton Houston and, 26, 30, 31
      Margold Report and, 29–30
      Thurgood Marshall and, 26, 30, 32
      role of the Garland Fund in, 27–29
      white Southerner's views of, 12–13
Civil Rights Act of 1866, 58
civil rights movement
   black nationalism and, 72
   black political representation
      1964 Democratic National Convention and, 65–70
      criticized by Malcolm X, 78
   John F. Kennedy and, 54–55
   "Letter from Birmingham Jail," 48–53, 55–56, 91–101
   March on Washington, 56
   nonviolent confrontation
      in Birmingham protests, 45–46, 53–54
      Martin Luther King and, 42, 43–45, 50–51
      in Montgomery Bus Boycott, 43–45
   role of the Student Nonviolent Coordinating Committee in, 61
   voter registration campaigns, 57–58, 60–61, 62–65
Civil War. *See* Emancipation Proclamation
Clark, Kenneth B., 32–33, 34, 77
clergy
   criticism of King's Birmingham protests, 46–48
Cleveland, Grover, 22
COFO. *See* Council of Federated Organizations
Commager, Henry Steele, 12
Commissions on Race, 56
Cone, James H., 42, 48, 75–76, 84

Conner, Eugene "Bull," 45, 46, 53, 54
Cotton States and International Exposition. *See* Atlanta Exposition
Council of Federated Organizations (COFO), 57, 61
Creelman, James, 22

Davis, John W., 35–36
Davis et al. v. County School Board of Prince Edward County, Virginia, 32
Declaration of Independence, 42–43
Delany, Martin, 73–74
Democratic National Convention
   of 1964, 65–70
      Fannie Lou Hamer's testimony at, 66–68, 102–105
   of 1968, 70
Dittmer, John, 67
Douglass, Frederick, 13, 58
Drew, Timothy. *See* Ali, Noble Drew
Du Bois, W. E. B.
   black voting rights and, 59–60
   criticism of Booker T. Washington and accommodationist strategies, 23–24
   life and career of, 24

Eastland, James, 40
Easy Burden, An (Young), 71
Eisenhower, Dwight D., 37
Emancipation Proclamation, 8

Fard, Wallace D., 75
Fifteenth Amendment, 26
   black voting rights and, 8, 57, 58
Forman, James, 61
Fourteenth Amendment, 8, 26, 58
   Thurgood Marshall on, 36, 37–38
Frankfurter, Felix, 29, 30, 35
Freedmen's Bureau, 13, 14
freedom schools, 62
Freedom Summer, 62

Gandhi, Mohandas K. "Mahatma," 43, 44
Garland, Charles, 27
Garland Fund, 27–29, 30
Garvey, Marcus, 34, 73, 74
Gebhart v. Belton, 32
"good character clause," 10
"grandfather clause," 11
Guardian (Boston newspaper), 22–23

Hamer, Fannie Lou
   advocacy of black voting rights, 57
   arrested and beaten in jail, 65
   death of, 70

at the Democratic National Convention
 of 1968, 70
legacy of, 70–71
Mississippi Freedom Democratic Party
 and, 66, 69–70
runs for political office, 65
testimony at the 1964 Democratic
 National Convention, 66–68
 Lyndon Johnson's response to, 68
 national response to, 68–69
 text of, 102–105
voter registration campaigns
 involvement in, 65
 motivated by, 57–58, 61, 63–65
Hampton Normal and Industrial Institute,
 14–15
Harding, Vincent, 41
Harris, Thomas E., 24
higher education, challenges to
 segregation in, 30, 32
Houston, Charles Hamilton, 26, 29, 30, 31
Howard University Law School, 30, 31

"I Have a Dream" speech. *See* King,
 Martin Luther, Jr.
integration
 criticized by
  black nationalists, 72, 74
  Malcolm X, 78–79
International Convention of Negro
 Peoples of the World, 74
Irons, Peter, 32, 33–34, 39
Islam
 black nationalism and, 74–75
 Nation of Islam and, 76–77

Jet (magazine), 68
Jim Crow laws, 9–10
Johnson, Lyndon B., 68, 82
Jones, Clarence, 47, 49

Kennedy, John F., 54–55, 79
King, Martin Luther, Jr.
 Andrew Young and, 71
 assassination of, 56
 Birmingham protests and, 45–53, 54
 "I Have a Dream" speech, 56
  criticized by Malcom X, 78
 influences on, 42–43
 "Letter from Birmingham Jail," 42,
  48–53
  on defying unjust laws, 51–52
  on direct action, 50–51
  on extremism, 52–53
  on the fight for civil rights, 49–50
  significance and legacy of, 54, 55–56

text of, 91–101
 writing of, 48–50
Malcolm X and, 78, 81
March on Washington, 56
Mississippi Freedom Democratic Party
 and, 66
Montgomery Bus Boycott, 43–45
nonviolent confrontation and, 43–45
voter registration drives and, 60
Andrew Young and, 71
King, Martin Luther, Sr., 42
Kluger, Richard, 29

Langston, John Mercer, 58
lawyers, as social engineers, 30
Lee, Chana Kai, 63–64, 65
legal briefs, 38
Legal Defense Fund (LDF), 26, 32, 34
"Letter from Birmingham Jail." *See* King,
 Martin Luther, Jr.
Liberian Exodus Joint Stock Steamship
 Company, 74
Lincoln, Abraham, 8
Lord, Nathalie, 15

Mackie, Mary F., 15
Malcolm X
 assassination of, 84–85
 "The Ballot or the Bullet" speech,
  79–83
  text of, 101–102
 on black militancy, 77–78
 black nationalism and, 72
 change in attitude toward whites,
  83–84
 criticism of mainstream civil rights
  movement and integration, 78–79
 on hate, 77
 moderation of viewpoints, 79
 in the Nation of Islam, 76, 77
 pilgrimage to Mecca, 83
 pride of being black, 77
 significance of, 85
 split from Nation of Islam, 79
 March on Washington, 56
  criticized by Malcolm X, 78
Margold, Nathan Ross, 29–30
Margold Report, 29–30
Marshall, Thurgood
 Brown v. the Board of Education and,
  26
 arguments before the Supreme
  Court, 34–36, 37–38
 text of closing arguments, 89–91
 evidence on the psychological
  effects of segregation, 32–34

challenges to segregation in higher
  education, 30
 on Charles Hamilton Houston, 31
 Legal Defense Fund and, 26, 32
Martin Luther King Day, 56
Mecca, 83
Meharry Medical College, 30
Meltzer, Milton, 13
MFDP. See Mississippi Freedom
  Democratic Party
militancy
 black nationalism and, 72
 Malcolm X on, 77–78, 83
Mississippi
 Fannie Lou Hamer runs for office in, 65
 voter registration
  drives in, 57–58, 60–63, 65
  procedure, 64
Mississippi Freedom Democratic Party
  (MFDP), 66, 68, 69–70
Montgomery Bus Boycott, 43–45
Moorish Science Temple of America, 75
Moors, 75
Morris, Charles Satchel, 24
Moses, Robert Parris, 61–63
Muhammad, Elijah, 75, 76, 79
Murray, Donald, 32
Muslim Mosque, Inc., 79

NAACP. See National Association for the
  Advancement of Colored People
National Association for the Advancement
  of Colored People (NAACP), 26
 black voting rights and, 57
 Brown v. the Board of Education and,
  32–38
 challenges to segregation in higher
  education, 30, 32
 Charles Hamilton Houston and, 30, 31
 focus on middle-class blacks, 73
 founding of, 59–60
 Garland Fund and, 27
 legal strategies to advance civil rights,
  26–30, 31
 Margold Report and, 29–30
 W. E. B. Du Bois and, 24
National Council of Churches (NCC),
  55–56
National Equal Rights League, 58
National Urban League (NUL), 73
Nation of Islam
 founding of, 75
 Malcolm X in, 76, 77
 splits from, 79
 messages of hope and self-sufficiency

  to blacks, 76–77
 views of whites, 75–76
NCC. See National Council of Churches
Negro World, The (newspaper), 73
Niagara Movement, 24, 59
Nigeria, 73
nonviolent
 commitment card, 48
 confrontation
  Birmingham protests, 45–46, 53–54
  Gandhi and, 43, 44
  Martin Luther King and, 43–45
  "Letter from Birmingham Jail," 42,
   50–51
  Montgomery Bus Boycott, 43–45
North Star, The (abolitionist newspaper),
  13
NUL. See National Urban League

OAAU. See Organization of Afro-
  American Unity
Organization of Afro-American Unity
  (OAAU), 84

Parks, Rosa, 43
Plessy v. Ferguson, 26, 29, 31
poll taxes, 10
Poole, Elijah. See Muhammad, Elijah

Radical Republicans, 58
Reagan, Ronald, 56
Rebel, The (Camus), 62
rebellion
 Camus on, 62
 Robert Parris Moses and, 62–63
Reconstruction, 8, 73
Robinson, Reginald, 61
Rockefeller, John D., 22
Roosevelt, Theodore, 22

Salley, Columbus, 31
Satyagraha, 44
school segregation
 legal challenges to
  Brown v. the Board of Education,
   26, 32–41
  focus of the NAACP on, 30
  in higher education, 31, 32
  role of the Garland Fund in, 28–29
 psychological effects of, 32–34
 "separate but equal" philosophy, 28
SCLC. See Southern Christian
  Leadership Conference
Shabazz, James, 84
Sipuel, Ada, 32
Sipuel v. University of Oklahoma Board of

Regents, 32
slavery. See Emancipation Proclamation
Souls of Black Folks, The (Du Bois), 23, 24, 59
Southern Christian Leadership Conference (SCLC)
   Birmingham children's protest, 53
   formation of, 45
   Robert Parris Moses and, 62
   voter registration drives and, 60
   Andrew Young and, 71
Stride Toward Freedom (King), 43
Student Nonviolent Coordinating Committee (SNCC)
   Fannie Lou Hamer and, 65
   freedom schools and, 62
   involvement in the civil rights movement, 61
   Robert Parris Moses and, 61–63
   voter registration drives in Mississippi, 60–63, 65
Sugarman, Tracy, 68–69
Supreme Court, U.S.
   Brown v. the Board of Education, 26
   arguments by opposing sides, 34–38
   text of Marshall's closing arguments, 89–91
   unanimous decision in, 38–39
   Earl Warren appointed to, 37
   how cases are argued before, 38
   in legal strategies for civil rights, 27
   Margold Report and, 29–30
   Plessy v. Ferguson, 26, 29, 31
   Sipuel v. University of Oklahoma Board of Regents, 32

Talmadge, Eugene, 40
Thirteenth Amendment, 8
Thomas Aquinas, Saint, 51
Thoreau, Henry David, 43
trade schools, 13.
   see also vocational training
Trotter, William Monroe, 22–23
Turner, Henry McNeal, 74
Tuskegee Institute, 16–17
Tuskegee Movement, 17
Tuskegee University, 16

"understanding clause," 10
UNIA. See Universal Negro Improvement Association
Universal Negro Improvement Association (UNIA), 73, 74
University of Maryland, 32

Vinson, Chief Justice, 37
violence
   Malcolm X on, 77–78, 83
vocational training
   advocates of, 12–14, 18–19
   Tuskegee Institute, 16–17
voter registration
   campaigns
   influence on Fannie Lou Hamer, 57–58, 61, 63–65
   Robert Parris Moses and, 61, 62–63
   organized in Mississippi, 57–58, 60–63, 65
   procedure in Mississippi, 64
voting rights. See black voting rights

Warren, Earl, 26
   appointed to the Supreme Court, 37
   decision in Brown v. the Board of Education, 38–39
Washington, Booker T.
   accommodationist views, 12, 13
   advocacy of vocational training, 12
   "Atlanta Compromise" speech, 18–22, 25
   at the Atlanta Exposition, 12, 17–22
   black voting rights and, 59
   "Cast Down Your Bucket" speech, 18–22, 25
   text of, 86–89
   criticism of, 22–24
   at the Hampton Normal and Industrial Institute, 14, 15
   influence of, 22
   later views of, 24–25
   on Samuel Chapman Armstrong, 15
   Tuskegee Institute and, 16–17
   Wayland Seminary and, 15–16
Wayland Seminary, 15–16
White, Walter, 29, 30
whites
   Malcolm X's attitudes toward, 83–84
   viewed by Nation of Islam, 75–76
Whitten, Jamie, 65
Why We Can't Wait (King), 49
Williams, Juna, 35
World War I, 60

Young, Andrew, 70, 71

Picture Credits

Cover Photo: © Bettmann/Corbis
Agence France Presse/Archive Photos, 53
© Bettmann/Corbis, 36, 39, 46, 51, 66, 68, 69
© Corbis, 73
John F. Kennedy Library, 55
Library of Congress, 10, 12, 16, 17, 19, 20, 23, 25, 28, 31, 33, 34, 35, 37, 44, 47, 49, 52, 59, 61, 63, 71, 75, 76, 78, 79, 80, 83, 84
© Medford Historical Society Collection/Corbis, 15
North Wind Picture Archives, 9
Schomburg Center for Research in Black Culture, 27, 40, 72
© Flip Schulke/Corbis, 57

About the Author

Charles George was born and raised in a small town in western Texas. Growing up during the 1950s and 1960s, he experienced firsthand some aspects of the Jim Crow system. After graduating from Tarleton State University with a degree in Spanish and history, George taught in Texas public high schools for fifteen years. Most recently he was head of the Social Studies Department at Early High School in central Texas, but he has since taken a break from the classroom to write full time with Linda, his wife of twenty-eight years.

Together, they have written over thirty young adult and children's nonfiction books in the past two years, including two that dealt with the civil rights movement. Charles George and his wife currently live in the mountains of Southern New Mexico.